THE
LITTLE
BOOK
OF
HOGMANAY

BOB PEGG

First published 2013

The History Press
The Mill, Brimscombe Port
Stroud, Gloucestershire, GL5 2QG
www.thehistorypress.co.uk

British Library Cataloguing in Publication Data.
A catalogue record for this book is available from the British Library.

ISBN 978 0 7524 8964 3

Typesetting and origination by The History Press
Printed in Great Britain

CONTENTS

ACKNOWLEDGEMENTS

Tocher, the Scots word for dowry, is the title of a journal published by the Department of Celtic and Scottish Studies at Edinburgh University, with selections of oral, manuscript and photographic material from the School of Scottish Studies Archive. I am indebted to the department for permission to reference or reproduce excerpts on the following pages of the book. The volume number and contributor's name are given; a sound archive (SA) reference indicates the year these recordings were made. Especial thanks for help and advice to Archives Assistant Caroline Milligan.

page 19: *Tocher* 59, p.29, Graeme Mackinnon recorded by Emily Lyle SA1976.249.B1

page 77: *Tocher* 44, p.103, Dan Ralph recorded by Margaret Bennett and Gail Christey, SA1986.80A

page 101: *Tocher* 36-7, pp 358-361, conversation on New Year Guising in Lewis with Donald MacDonald, recorded by Alan Bruford SA1980.106

page 120: *Tocher* 12, p.138, divination custom from Islay. Maclagan mss, p.849

page 135: *Tocher* 8, pp 266-267, Annie Arnott, Skye, recorded by Calum Maclean, SA1953.10.A8; plus a note of a tradition about why the song was composed.

page 135: *Tocher* 16, pp 320-322, Peter Morrison, Grimsay, recorded by Donald A. MacDonald, SA1973.172.A3

page 135: *Tocher* 34, pp 252-255, Donald McColl, Applecross, recorded by Alan Bruford, SA1967.9.A1 and SA1975.57.A1

The poem *Hogmanay (To a Pipe Tune)* courtesy of the estate of Violet Jacob.

Manuscript account of the last shinty match on Iona, courtesy of the descendants of the Reverend Coll A. MacDonald.

Childhood song and anecdote from Hamish Imlach, from personal correspondence with Ewan McVicar.

Thanks for assistance to staff in the reference sections of Dingwall Library, Inverness Library and the National Library of Scotland; the British Newspaper Archive was also a useful online resource. Thanks also to Laura Smyth, librarian at the Vaughan Williams Memorial Library for directing me to Anne G. Gilchrist's article.

Thanks to my old friend John Hodkinson. Once again he has risen to the challenge, creating images whose resonance goes far beyond illustration.

My grateful thanks also to the following, for generously sharing stories, memories, wisdom, and a recipe: Mike Anderson, Elizabeth Brown, Zan Dunn, Arthur and Joan Dutch, Vonne Hammerstone, Janet MacInnes, Adam McNaughtan, Geordie McIntyre, Alison McMorland, Ewan McVicar, Jim Miller, Tom Muir, Lindsey Payne, Donald Smith, Sheila Stewart, Lawrence Tulloch, and Alec Williamson.

Finally much more than thanks must go to Mairi MacArthur. Without her scholarship, research skills and support, this book would simply not have come into existence.

INTRODUCTION

Today we agree to call the last day of the Scottish year 'Hogmanay', whose evening is celebrated in a very particular and distinctive way. Towards midnight, people with the will and the stamina gather together in homes, hotels, hostelries and halls; and outdoors in streets, parks, towns and cities – in the present case of Edinburgh in crowds of close to 100,000 individuals. There may be a ceilidh dance, a street concert – or, for those at home, a 'TV special'. Then come 'the Bells' – the universal term for the moment of transition between the Old Year and the New – and members of crowds link arms to sing *Auld Lang Syne*, or at least the song's first verse and chorus, then repeat the chorus with increasing rapidity until it becomes a wild chant. Drams may be taken, to top up the drink that has already been consumed, and New Year's Day will be spent, by some at least, recovering from Hogmanay excess.

Hogmanay nowadays is a highlight of a holiday period which begins at Christmas and continues through as far as 4 January, depending on where the weekends fall, though shops and supermarkets are kept open most of the time. But, in many parts of Scotland, people in their sixties and beyond will tell you that, when they were children, New Year alone was the time for midwinter celebration – with widespread first-footing, baking and special meals – and that Christmas was hardly recognised. This is not surprising, first because Christmas only became an official public holiday in Scotland in 1958, and second because it was banned as a festival by the Reformed Church in 1560. Despite the defiance of individuals and communities, and the relative laxity of the clergy in some places, it never recovered the vitality it had before it was proscribed. The contemporary Scottish Christmas is essentially the Victorian version – with the tree, the cards and

the wrapped presents – but, before the Reformation, Christmas was generally called Yule, which was also the name for a more extended period, a time of sometimes wild celebration which could last from several days before the feast of Christmas itself until well into January, when people would carouse, start fires, make special foods, and ramble the streets in disguise, to the alarm of more sober citizens.

After the banning of Christmas, many of the Yule customs connected to it were shifted into the New Year period, a time when seasonal celebrations were still relatively tolerated by the authorities. So, in Scotland, New Year became a melting pot for activities that had previously extended over a period of a couple of weeks or more, during which Hogmanay – *Oidhche Challuinn* in Gaelic – was just one pivotal point among a whole range of festivities.

In this book I want to look at the rich and varied ways in which Midwinter is still celebrated in Scotland, as well as going back in time to show what, in the past, was an enormous variety of activity, from Guising and New Year's Day sports, to divination and flaming tar barrels. Many different voices can be heard. Some speak in open disapproval, condemning practices they see as heathen or Popish; others report without comment; and there are those who openly celebrate customs which are a part of the lives of their own communities. Clergymen, antiquarians, lexicographers, folklorists, travellers, journalists, storytellers, singers and songwriters: what fine talk they would make at a Hogmanay gathering – if only they could be gathered together – exchanging old tales and personal reminiscences; and occasionally, to add spice to the rich black bun of conversation, disputing among themselves, as Presbyterian strictness at the one extreme wrangled with hedonistic devil-may-care at the other.

1

THE QUEST FOR HOGMANAY

Hogmana, hoguemennay, hagmenay, hug-me-nay, huigmanay, hagmonick, hangmanay, huggeranohni, hog ma nae; these are some of the configurations used over the past 450 years for that mysterious word we now agree to spell as 'Hogmanay'. But where does it come from, and what does it mean, with its embodiment of the spirit of the Caledonian New Year's Eve, when the Scots celebrate with whisky, music, dancing and good cheer, and the rest of the world is very welcome to join in, if it pleases?

Over the last couple of centuries, the origins and meaning of Hogmanay have been discussed at length, but never rooted out. There are just too many possibilities to choose from. With its variety of spellings, the word begins to crop up relatively frequently in the seventeenth century. During the following century, it was scrutinised by a growing body of antiquarians, and John Jamieson's *Etymological Dictionary of the Scottish Language*, which was published in two volumes in 1808 and 1809 – the dictionary itself a great feat of antiquarian scholarship – gives the meaning of 'Hogmanay' or 'Hogmenay' as 'the name appropriated by the vulgar to the last day of the year'. Jamieson adds that, in Northumberland, the month of December is called 'Hagmana', quotes from a late seventeenth-century account of 'plebeians in the South of Scotland' going about 'from door to door on New-year's Eve, crying Hagmane', and gives a further meaning as a New Year's Eve gift or entertainment. Jamieson then goes on to suggest possible origins of the word, from the Scandinavian 'Hoggu-not' or 'Hogenaf' – a Yule Eve night of animal slaughter – to the French 'Au gui menez', translated as 'to the mistletoe', a cry uttered in the sixteenth century by participants in the Fête de Fous (or Feast of Fools), a midwinter period of license and satirical mockery. Jamieson quotes from an article published in the *Caledonian Mercury* on 2 January 1792, which says that:

... many complaints were made to the Gallic Synods, of great excesses which were committed on the last night of the year, and on the first of January, during the *Fête de Fous*, by companies of both sexes, dressed in fantastic habits, who run about with their Christmas Boxes, called *Tire Lire*, begging for the lady in the straw, both money and wassels. These beggars were called *Bachelettes*, Guisards; and their chief *Rollet Follet*. They came into the churches, during the service of the vigils, and disturbed the devotions by their cries of *Au gui menez, Rollet Follet, Au gui menez, tiri liri, mainte du blanc et point du bis* ...

The derivations that Jamieson suggests are still offered today when the origins of the meaning of Hogmanay are discussed, and no scholar during the two centuries since his time has come up with a more plausible alternative; though a charming suggestion was made by John MacTaggart in *The Scottish Gallovidian Encyclopaedia* (1824). MacTaggart, from Kirkcudbrightshire, a farmer's son, only in his mid-twenties and largely self-educated, cheekily comments on John Jamieson's labours:

HOG-MA-NAY, or HUG-ME-NAY – The last day of the year. Dr. Jamieson, with a research that would have frightened even a Murray or a Scalinger to engage in, has at last owned, like a worthy honest man as he is, that the origin of this term is quite uncertain; and so should I say also, did I not like to be throwing out a hint now and then on various things, even suppose I be laughed at for doing so.

Then here I give, like myself, whom am a being of small scholarcraft, a few *hindish* speculations respecting this mystic phrase; to be plain, I think *hog-ma-nay* means *hug-me-now* – *Hawse and ney*, the old nurse term, meaning, 'kiss me, and I'm pleased,' runs somewhat near it: *ney* or *nay* may be a variation that time has made on now. Kissing, long ago, was a thing much more common than at present. People, in the days gone by, saluted [each] other in churches, according to Scripture, with *holy kisses*; and this smacking system was only laid aside when priests began to see that it was not *holiness* alone prompted their congregations to hold up their gabs to one another like *Amous dishes* as Burns says ...

At weddings too, what a kissing there was; and even to this day, at these occasions much of it goes on: and on the happy nights of *hog-ma-nay*, the kissing trade is extremely brisk, particularly in *Auld Reekie* [Edinburgh]; then the lasses must kiss with all the stranger lads they meet ...

From such causes, methinks, *hog-ma-nay* has started.
The *hugging day* the time to *hug-me-now*.

Perhaps in a similar spirit of mischief, Professor Ted Cowan, in an article in *The Scotsman* in 2005, proposes 'houghmagandie' – coolly defined in *The Concise Scots Dictionary* as 'fornication' – as at least a close relation, given the amount of kissing and general emotional warmth that the season generates.

Whatever the truth about the origins of Hogmanay – and what a splendid word it is, whatever its derivation – the links to the French Fête de Fous may be real enough, given the cultural closeness of France and Scotland during the Auld Alliance (1295–1560). Before the Reformation in Scotland, the Christmas – or Yule – period lasted from Christmas Eve or before until Twelfth Night and beyond. As in France and elsewhere, what in some parts of Scotland came to be called the Daft Days was a time when less inhibited folk would don disguises, cross-dress, and roam the streets singing, playing music, larking about, and generally making a racket.

In 1651 Oliver Cromwell, who was then occupying Edinburgh, had the English Parliament ban Christmas. In Scotland, however, the Reformed Church, on the look-out for anything that smacked

of Catholic 'superstition', had already abolished all feast and saints' days in their *First Book of Discipline* of 1560 on the grounds that they had no scriptural authority. This didn't, however, stop folk celebrating Midwinter in ways which had nothing to do with Christianity of any stripe. On 30 December 1598, Elgin Kirk Session records:

> George Kay accusit of dancing and guysing in the night on Monday last. He confesses he had his sister's coat upon him and the rest that were with him had claythis dammaskit about thame and their faces blackit, and they had a lad play upon banis [bones] and bells with them. Arche Hay had a faise [mask] about his loynes and a kerche about his face. Ordained to make repentance two Sundays bairfut and bairleggit.

The following year:

> Anent the Chanonrie Kirk. All prophane pastime inhibited to be usit be any persones ather within the burgh or college and speciallie futballing through the toun, snaw balling, singing of carrellis or uther prophane sangis, guysing, pyping, violing, and dansing and speciallie all thir above spect. forbidden in the Chanonrie Kirk or Kirk yard thairoff (except football). *All women and lassis forbiddin to haunt or resort thair under the paynis of publict repentans, at the leist during this tyme quhilk is superstitiouslie keipitt fra the xxv day of December to the last day of Januar nixt thairefter.*

Cross-dressing and disguise, street games, music, singing and dancing in the streets after dark are all aspects of the Scottish midwinter celebrations that the Church failed to suppress. Many of them have kept going, or, have faded out and then been revived, into the present day. But although the festivities of the Yule period did continue in some areas, the effect of banning Christmas and its associated customs and pastimes was to shift many of these activities to the New Year.

A switch to the Gregorian calendar in 1752 put New Year back eleven, and then twelve days. Many people felt aggrieved that they had been robbed of these days, and some communities continued to celebrate Christmas and New Year in the Old Style, eleven or twelve days later than their modernised neighbours. In 1883, Constance Gordon Cumming writes:

There is a further division of the winter festivals by the partial adoption of New Style in reckoning. Thus, just as one half of the people keep Hallowe-en on the last night of October and the others observe the 11th of November, so with the New Year. This is especially remarkable on the Inverness-shire and Ross-shire coasts, which face one another on either side of the Beauly Firth. Long before sunrise on the first of January, the Inverness hills are crowned with bonfires and, when they burn low, the lads and lassies dance round them and trample out the dying embers. The opposite coast shows no such fires till the morning of the New Year Old Style, when it likewise awakens before daylight to greet the rising sun.

The Ross-shire Journal for 4 January 1878 describes the success of local businessmen in persuading the citizens of Alness to observe calendrical changes made over 100 years previously:

Yesterday was observed by all as the New Year holiday. Even conservative Bridgend went heartily in for it. Mr MacKenzie, ironmonger, and Mr Munro, merchant, had visited every house in the town last week and explained to the people the absurdity of observing the 12th of January. All pledged themselves to holding the 1st and it happened as promised.

But the following year, on 8 January 1879, *The Ross-shire* published a mild reproof to those folk in Tain who were still holding on to the old ways:

A great many of the older people in Tain cling to the Old Style, holding a holiday on the 13th January, as this year the 12th fell on the Sabbath ... We do hope that this is the last occasion when it will have to be chronicled that New Year rejoicings were held at Tain twelve days behind the proper time.

For 900 years or so, until well into the nineteenth century, Gaelic was the everyday language of most people living north of the Highland line, and is still spoken widely in Skye and the Western Isles. Until this area was infiltrated linguistically by Scots and English, the word 'Hogmanay' wasn't used there at all for New Year's Eve. In Gaelic the New Year is *a'Challuinn*, New Year's Day *Calluinn*, and New Year's Eve *Oidhche Challuinn* (literally 'the night of New Year's Day').

The Ross-shire Journal again, in 1910, gives a brief but lively summary, this time without any reproach, of the New Year's Day activities in Gaelic-speaking Poolewe, in Wester Ross:

A'Challuinn. Thursday was observed as New Year's Day (Old Style) in most parts of the wide parish of Gairloch. The day was spent in the traditional fashion in visiting and greeting friends, Fingalian feasting, singing Gaelic songs and games of shinty. All the schools and places of business were closed. The children on the previous day, as usual, went their rounds with their bags and camans [shinty sticks] singing their 'Calluinn duans' [New Year poems or chants].

Later in these pages, Alec Williamson describes how, well into the twentieth century, the community in Easter Ross in which he was brought up was divided between the people of Edderton village who were members of the Church of Scotland and who celebrated Hogmanay on 31 December, and the people on the surrounding hill crofts who were Free Church members, and kept Old New Year's Eve on 11 January.

In Scotland, until not much over 100 years ago, New Year's Eve – Hogmanay, *Oidhche Challuinn* – was just the one day, though a very important day, in a whole seasonal cluster of custom and celebration. In a few places this season could extend from before Christmas (whether Old or New Style) until late January. More generally, though, celebrations were packed into a shorter period, and in those parts of Scotland where the proscription of Christmas had been particularly effective, it was not a special time, until recently. Shops would be open, and father would go to work, though he might come home early to enjoy a special meal. As noted above, Christmas Day wasn't a public holiday in Scotland until 1958, with Boxing Day following in 1974. Since then the modern, or rather Victorian, version of Christmas has pretty much universally taken hold.

People living today will also tell you that Hogmanay is not what it used to be, and this is true enough. The baking and the first-footing, which were widespread in the recent past, have been largely supplanted by an evening in front of the television, with drink taken long before the midnight Bells; while the young people who formerly might have gone round visiting are now drawn to celebrations organised for them on a mass scale. But reports of the decline of New Year customs, and complaints that Hogmanay isn't what it

was, go back well into the nineteenth century. Here is the beginning of a piece – set in the central Highlands – from *The Celtic Magazine*, published in 1875 under the pen name of 'Knockfin':

NEW YEAR IN THE OLD STYLE IN THE HIGHLANDS

Old Mr Chisholm sat at his parlour fire after a hearty New Year dinner. His wife occupied the cosy arm-chair in the opposite corner; and gathered round them were a bevy of merry grand-children, enjoying New Year as only children can. Their parents were absent at the moment, and the family group was completed by a son and daughter of the old couple.

Mr Chisholm was in a meditative mood, looking into the bright blazing fire.

'Well,' he observed at last with an air of regret, 'the New Year is not observed as it was when we were children, wife. It's dying out, dying out greatly. When these children are as old as we are there will be no trace of a Christmas or a New Year holiday. What did you say you had been doing all day Bill?' he asked, turning to his son.

'Shooting,' said Bill, 'and deuced cold I was. Catch me trying for the silver medal and other prizes another New Year's Day.'

'Shooting may be interesting,' said Mr Chisholm, 'but as you say it is cold work. We had sometimes a shot at a raffle in my young days, but usually we had more exciting business. Shinty my boy, shinty was our great game,' and Mr Chisholm looked as if he greatly pitied the degeneracy of the latter days.

'I have played shinty myself,' said Bill, 'and I see it is still played in Badenoch and Strathglass, and among wild Highlanders in Edinburgh. But it's too hard on the lungs for me, and besides we never play it here.'

'The more's the pity, Bill. There's no game ever I saw I could compare to shinty. Talk about cricket, that's nothing to it. Shinty was suited to a New Year's Day; it kept the spirits up and the body warm. I should like to have a turn at it yet; wouldn't I run?'

And the old man's heavy frame shook as he chuckled at the idea.

'However, there's no use speaking; is tea ready wife?'

'No, and it won't be for half-an-hour yet, perhaps longer,' said Mrs Chisholm. 'You know we have to wait for Bella and John,' indicating her married daughter and her husband.

'Then,' said the old man, 'come here bairns and I shall tell you how I spent one of my early New Year's Days.'

'Yes, do, grandfather,' shouted a happy chorus; 'now for a story.'

'Not much of a story,' replied Mr Chisholm, 'but such as it is you shall have it ...'

Mr Chisholm goes on to tell his grandchildren of a New Year's Day game of shinty, a sport we will engage with later.

In this book I have presented some of the stories not just of Hogmanay, but also, because they are an indivisible part of the same continuum, of the days that go before and after. But there is no denying that, for Scots all over the world, the day itself – particularly that moment when the Old Year ticks over into the New – is one to be celebrated, sometimes against the odds.

The great Orcadian explorer John Rae, working in the Arctic for the Hudson's Bay Company, recorded of midwinter 1846/47:

> On Christmas and New Year's Day a double allowance of fuel and flour was supplied. Fat venison steaks and plum pudding which a spirited game at foot ball gave a keen appetite, were the order of the day. A small supply of brandy from our scanty stock (3 Gallons) made the men feel quite happy, and I will venture to say that few merrier parties could be seen anywhere than they presented.

William Laing, an emigrant travelling to New Zealand on the *Bulworth* in 1859, stayed up with some companions making merry until eight bells – twelve o'clock – but then kept back a little drink until 5 a.m., when the Bells would have been heard in his native home. 'My thoughts are over the water,' he wrote in his journal. 'I can hear the city clocks of Aberdeen pealing forth the hour of midnight. I have my cup all ready, your good health then I wish.'

Writing in 1899, James McKerrow, in his *Reminiscences*, recalled his first New Year's Day in New Zealand in 1859, when he ate strawberries and cream in the warmth of the evening sun, missing the company of friends who would be sitting at the table by a cosy fire, sharing 'crisp oat cakes and ham, the buttered toast, the currant bun and the other fine things that make up a good Scotch tea', while, out in the night, the hail beat against the windows.

On 15 January 1918, the *Aberdeen Press and Journal* reported 'Stirring Scenes in Trench Caves', as the Gordon Highlanders:

... had quite a good time on Hogmanay night within 400 yards of the enemy. In some caves quarried deep below the trenches, they had a feast night and the spirit of Scotland moved among them and lived in their songs and speeches, with the memory of gallant comrades who had been with them a year ago and are no longer with them. The pipers came into the caves and their music filled those rocky vaults with wild sound, very haunting in its call to Scottish hearts, but it was imprisoned below ground and did not reach the German lines. The little dim light glowed on the steel helmets of the Gordons and made fantastic shadows on the walls as the pipers marched up and down, and shone in the eyes of the officers and men as they sipped hot rum punch and felt its warmth in their hearts.

The Glasgow Herald, on 1 January 1927, under the headline 'Hogmanay at Sea', reported elaborate plans for passengers crossing the Atlantic:

Preparations were made yesterday, prior to the sailing from the Clyde of the Anchor liner *Cameronia* with 400 passengers for Canada and the United States of America, for the celebration onboard of Hogmanay. Dinner and dancing parties were part of the programme and at midnight, when the liner would be well out to sea, it was arranged that passengers would assemble in the public rooms and sing Auld Lang Syne.

The importance of New Year, and, for many Scots, the insignificance of Christmas, is made clear in a story told by Graeme McKinnon, whose forbears emigrated to Victoria, Australia, in the 1870s. In an interview recorded in 1976 he recalled a particular Christmas Day in his youth when his father was too busy cutting oats on the farm to come home for Christmas dinner. That of course was a very important occasion for a nine-year-old boy, but Graeme continued:

I thought that showed devotion to his task but I was even more staggered when, on New Year's Day, exactly seven days later, when he was still in the midst of his harvest and there was a warning in the district that a locust plague was approaching which had every chance of wiping his oat crop out, he said, 'We are off to Maryborough for the

Highland Games.' I remember saying, 'But, dad, there are locusts coming.' And he said, 'It is the day for the Scots. It is the Highland Games. We are off.' And we drove through literally this tremendous plague of locusts which pulled us up. We had to stop and clean our radiator of the pests. And I've never forgotten that, that a man so devoted to his task would work through Christmas Day and yet New Year's Day being the Scotsman's day – that was his day of relaxation.

Lastly, here are the melancholy words written by 'Our Private Correspondent, London', and published in the *Inverness Courier* on 3 January 1850, expressing the longing for home of the stranger in a strange land. A long letter/column dated 31 December 1849 ends:

So I now wish you and your readers a blythe Hogmanay night and a happy new-year, both of which being little observed here as festive occasions I must endeavour to celebrate as I best can ... but aye remembering auld lang syne and its joyous appurtenances.

2

YULE

The town's bell rang through the dark of the winter morning with queer little jolts and pauses, as if Wanton Wully Oliver, the ringer, had been jovial the night before. A blithe New-Year-time bell; a droll, daft, scatter-brained bell; it gave no horrid alarums, no solemn reminders that commonly toll from steeples and make good-fellows melancholy to think upon things undone, the brevity of days and years, the parting of good company, but a cheery ditty – 'boom, boom, ding-a-dong boom, boom ding, hic, ding-dong,' infecting whoever heard it with a kind of foolish gaiety. The burgh town turned on its pillows, drew up its feet from the bed-bottles, last night hot, now turned to chilly stone, rubbed its eyes and knew by that bell it was the daftest of the daft days come.

These are the opening sentences of Neil Munro's novel *The Daft Days*, which was first published in 1907. In Scotland the Daft Days ('daft' here indicating frivolity and fun) corresponded roughly to Yule, which was not only the old term for Christmas, but could also signify a longer period, extending from Christmas (or before) well into January. The origins of the word are unknown, but it's said to be related to the Old English *Gēola* and the Old Norse *jól*, both of which were the names of midwinter festivals.

J. M. MacPherson, in *Primitive Beliefs in the Northeast of Scotland* (1929), calls the season the 'merry month', spent among the 'Northern peoples' in 'feastings, merry-makings, [and] bodily exercises'. MacPherson cites Elgin church records which imply that this period could have lasted from 25 December until the end of January. He goes on to suggest that, in the Moray area at least, there was a shorter period:

… which ended with a fire festival on Uphellya or Uphaliday, the last day of the Yule festivities. This was the thirteenth night of Yule and was the crowning event of the Yuletide revels.

This period of celebration ended with a cacophony of metal objects being hammered on through the streets, a practice banned in 1581 by Elgin borough council, which enacted a statute forbidding people to 'ring bassings, bells, or any other kind of brazen vessels or metals used of old on Uphellie Even'.

In spite of the council's efforts, folk were still banging on pots and pans more than fifty years later; in 1636 Alexander Dunbar was rebuked for 'clinking on basons throughout the town on Uphaly Even'.

The abolition of Christmas in Scotland by the Kirk (the Reformed Church) and later by Act of Parliament, was pretty effective, certainly in the Lowlands. In *Popular Rhymes of Scotland* (1841), Robert Chambers summarizes:

> Christmas and Twelfth Night, days so much observed in England, attract no regard in Scotland: the latter may be said to be not only unrecognised but unknown. This is no doubt owing to the persevering efforts made by the Presbyterian clergy, for a century after the Reformation, to extinguish all observance of Christmas. In the Highlands alone, and amongst Episcopalian families in large towns, is the festival of the Nativity held in any regard.

Chambers is right in suggesting that the Kirk's proscription hadn't been universally effective. Looking at Christmas and Yule customs that were kept up into the nineteenth century and later – in Fife and in Shetland, for example – it seems that the same practices to do with purification, visiting, feasting, licensed begging or charitable giving, disguise, divination and so on occurred both at Christmas and New Year, and, in some places, throughout the whole Yule period (however long that might have gone on for).

Reverend Walter Gregor, in *Notes on the Folk-Lore of the North-East of Scotland* (1881), says that, in that region, Christmas and New Year were kept with equal enthusiasm, with three days holiday or more over each period. Getting a blacksmith, for example, to work over Christmas was almost impossible unless there was an emergency like a broken meal mill, when human life might depend upon a speedy repair. Similarly, if work was started between Christmas and New Year, every attempt was made to get it finished before the next celebration began. Gregor's account of Christmas invokes a plethora of baking, larger than usual amounts of food being eaten (including the great wheel of cheese, the 'kebback'), prognostication, visiting and Guising, all of which were aspects of the New Year in places where Christmas was no longer celebrated:

> The whole time around Christmas and the New Year was given up to festivity to a greater or less degree. All the straw for the cattle had to be in readiness, and for several weeks before Christmas an additional hour was given to the 'flail.' Food and drink of all kinds were laid in store. 'Yeel' [Yule] fish was bought. Sometimes this was done from fisherwomen

who carried them over the country. Sometimes those in better circumstances went to the fishing villages, and bought the fish from the boat, carried them home, cured them, and smoked them on the kiln. The 'Yeel kebback' had been prepared a long time before, and the ale had been brewed more generously than usual, and was in its prime. Omens were drawn from the way in which the wort boiled. If the wort boiled up in the middle of the pot, there was a 'fey' person's drink in the pot. Bread of various kinds, 'bannocks,' 'soor cakes,' 'cream cakes,' 'facet cakes,' 'soft cakes,' was stored up. At the baking of the Yeel bread a cake was baked for each member of the family, and omens of the lot of the one for whom it was baked during the coming year were drawn. If the cake broke, it was looked upon as foreboding death. If only a piece of it broke off, bad health was augured. It was a habit to keep part of the Yeel cakes as long as possible, and they have been kept for weeks and months. It was thought lucky to do so. It was esteemed very unlucky to count at any time the number of cakes baked. The saying was 'there wis nae thrift in coontit cakes, as the fairies ate the half o' them.' For a household to have wanted ale, or fish, or a kebback, was looked upon as a forerunner of calamity during the coming year …

The first part of the festival consisted of 'Yeel sones.' This dish was prepared any time between Christmas Eve and an early hour on Christmas morning. Companies of the young friends of the household were invited to attend, and it was a common practice for some of them, after partaking of the dish in one house, to proceed to another, and then another, and another.

Small basins or wooden 'caps' or cogs were ranged in a row, into which the 'sones' was poured. Into one dish the cook secretly dropped a ring – betokening marriage; into another, a button – the emblem of a single life; and into a third, a sixpence – the token of widowhood. Each guest then chose a basin, a cap, or a cog …

On Christmas Eve a few of the more sportive of the youth in the villages went along the streets, and besmeared doors and windows with sones. Others disguised themselves, and went in companies of three and four, singing, shouting, and rapping at doors and windows. The houses whose inmates were known to them they entered with dancing, antic gestures, and all kinds of daffing. They were called 'gysers.'

'Sones' – sowans – is a sour porridge made from the fermented liquid of oat husks, and considered good for both body and soul.

An important day during the Yule period was Handsel Monday. It was the first Monday after New Year, and was celebrated into the twentieth century. In some places it was the main holiday of the midwinter season, rather than Christmas or New Year. Servants were generally given the day off and provided with a special tea, or given gifts such as money or tobacco. Children received presents too, and might go around the shops carolling, 'Now our songs we've sung, gie's our hansel and let us run', to be rewarded by the shopkeepers with fruit and cakes. The animals on the farm were given a little more feed than usual. This could also be a New Year custom, as Robert Burns acknowledges in his paean to a faithful horse, *The Auld Farmer's New-Year-Morning Salutation to his Auld Mare, Maggie. On giving her the accustomed ripp of corn to hansel in the new-year*, which begins:

A Guid New-year I wish thee, Maggie!
Hae, there's a ripp to thy auld baggie:
Tho' thou's howe-backit now, an' knaggie,
I've seen the day
Thou could hae gaen like ony staggie,
Out-owre the lay.

Handsel Monday was also a time for sport. In Aberlady, East Lothian, where at the beginning of the nineteenth century it was the chief winter holiday, there was quoits and shooting in the morning and foot racing and putting the shot in the afternoon, followed by a shinty match, which in later times was replaced by golf.

The Statistical Account of Scotland (1795) for Tillicoultry, Clackmannanshire, reports:

It is worth mentioning that one William Hunter, a collier, was cured in the year 1758 of an inveterate rheumatism or gout, by drinking freely of new ale, full of barm or yeast. The poor man had been confined to his bed for a year and a half, having almost entirely lost the use of his limbs. On the evening of *Handsel Monday*, as it is called... some of his neighbours came to make merry with him. Though he could not rise, yet he always took his share of the ale, as it passed round the company, and in the end he became much intoxicated. The consequence was, that he had the use of his limbs next morning, and was able to walk about. He lived more than 20 years after this, and never had the smallest return of his old complaint.

In Shetland the midwinter celebrations were much more protracted than in other parts of the north, and they were referred to in the plural, as 'the Yules'. Jessie Saxby was born on the island of Unst in 1842, the daughter of Eliza Air and Laurence Edmonston, a doctor who was also a pioneer conservationist. She was widowed in 1873 and supported herself and her six children as a prolific and successful writer. Her description of the Yules is taken from *Shetland Traditional Lore* of 1933 (though it is very close to her account in *The Home of a Naturalist*, which was published in 1888). Mixing a storyteller's invention with the observation of the folklorist, she portrays a season of celebration infused with caution; for this was the time when the Trows – 'the peerie Hill-men' – were abroad, visiting the world of mortals in search of human wives:

> The Yules began with Tulya's E'en which was seven days before Yule Day. On that night the Trows received permission to leave their homes in the heart of the earth and dwell, if it so pleased them, above the ground.
>
> One of the most important of all Yule observances was the sainin required to guard life and property from the Trows. At dayset on Tulya's E'en two straws were plucked from the stored provender and laid in the form of a cross at the stiggie (style) leading to the yard where the stacks of corn and hay were kept. A hair from the tail of each cow, or other beast about the place, was pleated and fastened above the byre door; and a 'lowan taund' (blazing peat) was carried through all out-houses.

Tulya's E'en was followed by Helya's Night, then came Tammasmas E'en, five nights before Yule Day:

> The evening was considered peculiarly given to rest. No work was done after dayset – unlike all other evenings of Yuletide. No amusements were allowed. The smallest deviation from what was orthodox on this occasion was sure to bring bad luck ...
>
> The Sunday preceding Yule Day was called Byaena's Day. That day half a cow's head was boiled and eaten for supper. The fat skimmed off the water was made with bursteen (highly dried oatmeal) into brose. The skull was cleaned and a candle stuck in the eye socket, and then it was set aside to be lighted and carried through the house and byre on Yule morning. If a cow's skull was not available then any beast's skull was substituted.

Though a family might be very poor they always contrived to have a morsel of 'flesh mate' to cook on Yule E'en. The kind neighbours saw to that.

There was a man and his wife who were of a sullen, quarrelsome nature, so much so that all the folk of their Isle gave them a wide berth. But on Yule E'en the Trows came and hung a buggie on their door-'lifter' containing a good few Yule 'mercies', and the neighbours laughed and said: 'Weel, weel! it's a mercy that even a Trow has the heart to mind auld Abie and his ill-vanded wife.' And the old pair boasted that they had good friends among the Trows, so that they need not care what the neighbours said or did. And the neighbours gossiped about it and laughed the more. Old Abie's buggie was the standing Yule joke of that toon for many years.

Yule cakes were made especially for each member of the household; they were round, pinched into points around the outer edge and a hole was made in the centre. People washed themselves all over, and put on clean clothes, and the house was thoroughly tidied:

All locks were opened, a lamp was left burning all night, and an 'iron blade weel scored' was ostentatiously exposed near the door, in case the Trows were coming that way.

On Yule morning, the gudeman of the house got up while it was still dark, lit the candle which had been stuck in the eye socket of the skull, and went to the byre to feed the cattle giving them a little more than usual. Then he went round the house, and sometimes to the neighbours, proffering a dram with which even the children might dampen their lips:

Football was the amusement of the men while the brief day lasted, dancing and indoor games, with singing and recitations, were the fun of the evening.

Trows, being excessively fond of dancing, always tried to join in the dancing; but this they could only do in the guise of a mortal. Woe betide the man, woman, or child who had not been sained, and by that omission left for the Trows to personate.

There are numerous stories told of the mischief done at this period by the Trows, through the thoughtlessness of sceptical and foolhardy individuals.

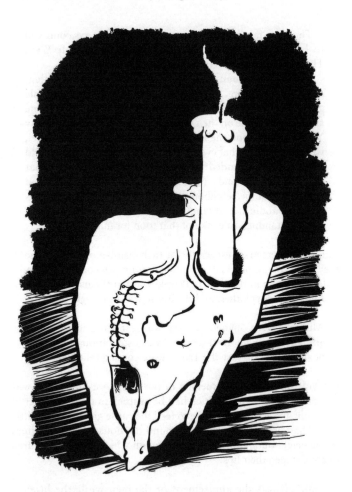

Working between Yule Day and New Year's Day brought bad luck. Two fishermen who went to sea on the fourth day of Yule, brought up 'a hideous monster, half-fish and half-horse', which pronounced:

Man that fished in Yule week
Fortune never mair did seek.

On Neuersday, work of every kind was begun. Men fished, if only for an hour (from a crag if too stormy to use a boat). Girls began a bit of knitting, if only a few stitches; a yard of

'simmond' (straw rope) was woven, a turf turned, a stone set
up, a shilling laid by, a torn garment mended and a new one
shaped, the byre was redd-up, fishing gear was repaired ...
From that day till 'Up-helly-a'' (twenty-fourth night) work
and play went hand in hand ...

On the evening of the twenty-fourth night young people came
together for dancing, in the house of someone who owned a big barn:

On 'Up-helly-a'' shortly before midnight doors were
opened and a great deal of pantomimic chasing, driving
and dispersing of unseen creatures took place. Many pious
ejaculations were uttered, and iron was again much in
evidence, 'fur, ye ken, Trows canna bide the sicht o' iron.'

The Bible was read and quoted. People moved about in
groups or couples, never singly, and infants were most
carefully guarded as well as sained by vigilant wise wives.
Young men and boys disguised as Grüliks [wearing tall,
beribboned straw hats, and with their faces veiled] formed
processions and marched through the toons with lighted
torches. These at midnight were piled with other material into
a huge bonfire, and amid noise and hearty congratulations
the Trows were banished to their homes in the hillsides.

When day dawned after the twenty-fourth night every
Trow had disappeared and the Yules were ended.

In a more recent account of the Yules, Lawrence Tulloch, storyteller, author, tour guide and retired lighthouse keeper, recalls a Shetland childhood on the island of Yell:

My earliest memories of Jül go back to the late 1940s. Christmas was regarded as a very important event but there was never a long drawn out lead up to it. In Shetland December is the darkest month of the year and there is no fishing and very little outside work done in a crofting community.

In the home the kitchen was the most important room. It was here that food was cooked and eaten and it was in the kitchen that folk sat around the fire in the evenings. Around the middle of the month, in preparation for Christmas, the women would undertake a very thorough clean. Paintwork was washed down as well as the ceiling. Often paintwork was renewed and the ceiling given a coat of distemper. Sometimes they hung fresh wallpaper and if the floor covering, lino, was shabby that was renewed as well.

In those days my aunt, Netta, was young and unmarried; she and my cousin John, who also lived with us, would decorate the kitchen. Crepe paper streamers and balloons were hung up along with the many cards that we got from friends and relations.

My father would kill the fatted hug. This was an adult sheep; as a ram lamb it had been castrated and reared. Several of those could be found on any croft. They were kept as excellent eating for the family or perhaps because the market was poor. No part of this beast was wasted; some of the entrails were eaten as tripe and some were stuffed and made into fruit puddings to be fried. The head was considered the tastiest part of all and the meat from it would be shared.

In midwinter there are no insects, no flies or bluebottles, and if the meat was hung up in a cool place there was no danger of it going off before it was all eaten. I assume that my parents set aside money for Christmas but, in our house, money was scarce. As well as my mother and father and me, there was my grandmother, her sister, Netta, and John, and there was very little income. My aunt Agnes was in hospital because she had TB. She was in hospital continuously for twenty years.

Nonetheless there were many things bought from the local shops that we never had at other times. Oranges were the delicious ones with thick skins, and apples were much enjoyed too. It was English apples that were favoured, and if a customer was allowed to select from the box in the shop they always shook an apple to assess its quality. If they could not hear the seeds rattle then it would be discarded in favour of another.

Of course a Christmas dram had to be bought; whisky, port, sherry and perhaps a few bottles of beer. With everything still rationed it was often what was available, as well as what could be afforded. For those who were teetotal there was ginger cordial and two tiny bottles, one with essence of peppermint and one with lavender. A few drops were carefully put on sugar cubes and offered as an alternative. This treat might be given at any time of year.

On Christmas Eve last minute preparations were made. Women would do final housework and men would bring into the barn extra feed for animals that were kept indoors during the winter. Later on Christmas Eve the men-folk would go in groups to visit. They would never pass a house that had a light in it, and it could be well into Christmas morning before they were finished.

Christmas Eve/Christmas morning was a time of high excitement for children looking for a visit from Santa Claus. The gifts that they got tended to reflect the financial well-being of the parents, though with almost every family being on equal footing there was sameness in what children got. Of course it depended how many children there were in a family and what ages they were. Always they got fruit, sweets, a cheap toy, and perhaps things that they needed in any event, like new boots, a new jumper, mittens, socks etc. I remember my uncle Bobby struggling to find the words to describe his excitement the year that he got a torch and batteries.

It was great entertainment for the youngsters seeing how the older men behaved when they had had a few drinks. Christmas was the only time of the year that many of them ever had drink. There was a kind of a code that a man drank what he was offered all at the one go. If a glass of whisky was accepted then something like this was said, 'since dus kom sae neer me nose, A'll tip de up an doon do goes'.

There would be singing and dancing, and anyone who could play the fiddle would be encouraged to do so. The following morning, after some sleep, and after animals had been fed and watered, visiting started up again, but this would be more local and less noisy.

My grandmother, despite the fact that she was very religious, and generally took a dim view of drinking, always set a bottle of whisky on the breakfast table. Children were not banned from tasting alcohol. Poor folk had so little of the stuff that it never posed any threat to them.

Christmas dinner would be served in the early part of the afternoon, perhaps around 2 p.m. when the daylight would be all but gone. Roast mutton, root vegetables, followed by steamed pudding was popular.

In Out Skerries, in Shetland, everyone had the same Christmas dinner – salted pig's head made into cabbage soup. One elderly Skerries man told me that when they were doing a round of visiting on Christmas Day they never made any attempt to go home for dinner. With everyone having the same dinner they simply ate wherever they happened to be at dinnertime. Everywhere in Shetland people had salted and dried pork and mutton, also salted white fish and pickled herring.

Young men always required some kind of competition on Christmas Day. For many years in North Yell, football was the thing. The football was home-made. A pig's bladder was salted and cured and it would be inserted into hand stitched leather 'quarters'. It was blown up as hard as the man with the hardest blow could make it. A kind of preliminary competition might take place to see who could kick the ball highest in the air. They did not have a toss, they drew 'knotty' – in other words they drew straws. The two captains who emerged as leaders picked their sides and there was no limit on numbers. Rules were pretty basic but it was a foul to cross the opponent's bye line.

Looking back, one thing that I find interesting and somewhat puzzling was the relationship between Christmas and the Kirk. In my youth Christmas had no religious aspect whatsoever. In those days the Church of Scotland was extremely fundamentalist and was very influential in the community, but there were never such things as watch night services or Christmas Day services. Sunday observance was of paramount importance so if Christmas Day fell on a Sunday they simply shifted Christmas Day into the middle of the week. All sorts of things were done on Christmas Day that would never be allowed on a Sunday.

The term 'Boxing Day' was unknown, but it was a day to try and get back to normal. The time until New Year was filled up in different ways. If the weather was good enough it might be possible to fish, that was a bonus, but some men would go the hills hunting rabbits.

I seem to recall that many promises were made to do even more visiting but this did not always happen.

In bygone days in Shetland the New Year tended to take second place to Jül – Christmas. It was never referred to as Hogmanay, indeed I never knew that word until I was near to being a teenager.

Some places in Shetland clung on to the Julian calendar, making New Year's Day the 12th of January. Nonetheless it was a time of drinking and feasting and no work was done save the feeding of animals and anything else essential.

On New Year's Eve all the men of the village would gather at the shop, a licensed grocer, to buy the necessary dram. Almost without exception they would buy two bottles of whisky, a bottle of port and one of sherry. One half of this stayed with the man and the rest was drams to have in the house for visitors. The men would divide into groups, perhaps a group of friends or perhaps neighbours, and they would set about visiting as many houses as possible. First-footing was no big deal although some men would want to take in the New Year in their own homes along with their families. Women never took part in the visiting process; it was not that there was any taboo; it was just that it meant that no house was empty of people.

The only section of the population who were uncomfortable with all this was the early teenagers, especially the boys. They too wanted to have bottles but they were too young, and their fathers would not have them in the group, it was for men not boys. Many resented staying at home with the women, so quite often they would go out Guising. They would dress up, sometimes cross-dress, wear masks and go visiting independently of the older men. Sometimes girls would go too and they all considered it great fun if the folk in the houses did not know who they were. All this went well into the small hours of the morning; every house would have an open door and if any household had gone to bed, that was no barrier to visitors. They would go straight to the bedrooms to offer drams and wish all and sundry a Happy New Year.

No matter how sore the heads were the following day, many men would turn out and make their way to the loch. To have some sort of a competition on Jül Day and New Year's Day was a long established tradition, and for many years the sailing of model yachts was all the rage. Yachts were nearly always home-made and they were sailed by pairs of men, one on either side of the loch. Every man would have a hip flask or half bottle, and spectators would gather in a sheltered spot to carry on where they left off the night before.

Even into modern times another important ritual that was always observed was to go to the sea. Christianity came to Shetland to stay around the year 1000 but older beliefs lingered. To Shetlanders the sea is so important that homage had to be paid to the sea gods. Even in the midst of festive celebrations they felt that they had to acknowledge the sea. On New Year's Day every householder would go to the shore and bring something back. It might be no more than a bucket of seawater to use in cooking or it might be a small quantity of crushed shells to give to the hens for grit, but it said in a loud, clear voice that we could never survive without the bounty that the sea provides year on year.

3

HOSPITALITY

Giving and receiving hospitality are at the heart of Hogmanay, and the exchange of food and drink is at the heart of that hospitality. Sometimes, in the past, the giving was only in one direction, when what was really licensed begging could help to fill the larders of poorer families at a lean time of the year.

Robert Chambers was born in the border town of Peebles in 1802. When he was sixteen years old he walked to Edinburgh with his brother William, and set up a book stall in Leith. He and William established an enormously successful publishing business, catering to the Victorian thirst for knowledge and self-improvement. Robert became a great gatherer and publisher of Scottish folklore, including accounts – some of them first-hand – of seasonal customs. In an article published in the periodical *The Olio, Or, Museum of Entertainment* in 1832 (which he later reworked for publication in his own books) he writes:

> In the town of Fife, which being quite secluded from other places, maintains old customs with considerable purity, the children of the poorer people – all of them without exception of sex or age, if only able to walk – get themselves at an early hour, tied into large aprons or sheets, the lower corners of which are turned up in front, so as to form each into a vast pocket or refectory. Thus rigged out, they go in families or bands to the doors of all the better sort of people, to collect an alms of oaten bread, from time out of mind accustomed to be given on this day by the rich to the poor. Each child gets one quadrant section of oat-cake, (some-times, in the case of particular favourites, improved by an addition of cheese), and this is called their *hogmanay*. In expectation of the large demands thus

made upon them, the housewives busy themselves, for several days beforehand, in preparing a suitable quantity of cakes ... The children on coming to the door cry, 'Hogmanay!' which is in itself a sufficient announcement of their demands; but there are other exclamations which either are or might be used for the same purpose. One of these is:

'Hogmanay,
Trollolay,
Give us some of your white bread, and none of your grey.'

Chambers then goes on confess that he has no idea of the meaning of the word 'Hogmanay', let alone 'Trollolay', and refers the reader to the kind of antiquarian discussion cited in Jamieson's *Dictionary*. He continues:

Of the many other cries appropriate to the morning of Hogmanay, I may chronicle two of the less puerile:
'Get up, goodwife, and shake your feathers,
And dinna think that we are beggars;
For we are bairns come out to play,
Get up and gie's our Hogmanay!'

Another is of a moralising character, though a good deal of a truism:
'Get up, goodwife, and binna sweir,
And deal your bread to them that 's here;
For the time will come when ye'll be dead,
And then ye'll neither need ale nor bread.'

She is in a very peevish strain, but, as saith the sage, 'Blessed is he that expects little for he will not be disappointed':
'My shoon are made of hoary hide;
Behind the door I downa hide
My tongue is sair I daurna sing –
I fear I will get a little thing.'

The most favourite of all, however, is much smarter, more laconic, and more to the point than any of the foregoing:
'My feet's cauld, my shoon's thin;
Gie's my cakes, and let me rin!'

It is no unpleasing scene, during the forenoon, to see the children going laden home, each with his large apron bellying out before him, stuffed full of cakes, and perhaps scarcely able to waddle under the load. Such a mass of oaten alms is no inconsiderable addition to the comfort of the poor man's household, and tends to make the season still more worthy of its jocund title.

Some of these rhymes have a decent history. This verse appeared in 1567, in *The Gude and Godlie Ballatis*. Here, the man of the house is entreated not to be idle:

O man, ryse up and be not sweir,
Prepare agains the gude new year;
My new year gift thou hes in stoir,
Gif me thy hart, I ask no moir.

And, in the twentieth century, children were still invoking the shaking out of the feather mattress cover, long after it had fallen out of general use; in *The Lore and Language of Schoolchildren* (1977), Iona and Peter Opie print this rhyme, very close to one given by Chambers, which a boy in Forfar used in the second half of the twentieth century for begging on Guy Fawkes night and other occasions, as well as at Hogmanay:

Rise up, auld wives, and shake yer feathers,
We're no come here as tinks or beggars,
We're only wee bairnies oot tae play,
So see oor pennies and let's away.

The Opies also cite a rhyme from a girl in Kirkcaldy, virtually identical to Chambers:

Ma feet's cauld, ma shin's [shoon] thin,
Gie's ma cakes an' let me rin.

Sometimes the collecting of food and alms would be on behalf of the old or poor of the community. Reverend Walter Gregor, minister for Pitsligo, was respected by fellow folklorists in the latter half of the nineteenth century as a collector who represented local traditions without Romantic embellishment. He was at one with his peers in feeling an urgency to set down old traditions before they died out:

Everything is changing, and changing faster than ever. The scream of the railway whistle is scaring away the witch, and the fairy, and the waterkelpie, and the ghost. To give an account of the olden time in the North, as seen by myself and as related to me by the aged, is the task I have set before me.

Reverend Gregor (1881) tells of the good works of the 'thiggers', companies of young men 'in twos, threes, and fours' who set out after breakfast on New Year's morning, 'to 'thigg' for an old woman, old man, aged couple, or an invalid that might be in narrow circumstances.' They carry a sack to collect meal, and a small bag for money, and sing a song which includes lines very like those in some of the children's rhymes above, as well as resembling songs sung by Guisers in Orkney and Shetland:

> The guide new year it is begun,
>> B' soothan, b' soothan.
> The beggars they're begun to run,
>> An awa b' mony a toon.
> Rise up gueedewife, an dinna be sweer,
>> B' soothan, b' soothan,
> An deal yir chirity t' the peer,
>> An awa b' mony a toon …

It's nae for oorsels it we come here,
  B' soothan, b' soothan,
It's for … sae scant o' gear,
  An awa b' mony a toon …
The roads are slippery, we canna rin,
  B' soothan, b' soothan,
We maun myne oor feet for fear we fa',
  An rin b' mony a toon.

After their song was done, the thiggers were invited into the house, and, declining to be seated, would take some whisky and cheese, then continue to go from dwelling to dwelling, gathering meal and money that would be doled out to 'many a poor old worthy'.

While, for the poor, New Year alms gave the opportunity to stock up the larder a little, for better-off folk it could be a time which offered at least the possibility of abundant good cheer. At the end of the eighteenth century the Strathmiglo weaver poet, Alexander Douglas, addresses his father-in-law, a shoemaker, and family, in *A New Year's Wish*:

I wish you all a gude new year,
  Wi' heart baith leal and canty;
May cheese an' bread, (the poor folks cheer,)
  Be in your amrie plenty;
A kebbuck too, like barrow-wheel,
  For time o' need reservin',
Fat brose, a ten-pint kag o' ale;
  Auld use an' wont observin'
    This new-year's day.

Douglas goes on to wish for even more bounty in the larder, including beef, haggis, 'a caller codlin', fresh from the sea – ham that 'three inch thick o' fat is…' and 'a string o' puddins in the lum', hanging up to smoke; as well as potatoes, meal, barley, peas, and beans.

Hogmanay continued to be the time for a special meal. Shepherd Willie Scott, born in 1897 and a renowned traditional singer, recalled going from house to house on Auld Year's Nicht in the Borders:

We aa met at the gamekeeper's hoose first, his wes the lowest hoose in the top o the valley … an there were a dram an ee got a bit cake an sang a sang. Ye'd go mebee fifty or sixty

yairds up an across the bridge an ee were received there. Well, he wes ma boss, so he mostly gave us a bottle o whisky away wi us. Then we went tae anither place an he'd gie us oor supper, pigeon pie. There were a lot o pigeons aboot the place an he always got them shot and made a big pie, o as big as a small table y'know. Ye got a pigeon apiece, the legs were stickin oot o the top o the crust.

Poet and storyteller Janet MacInnes remembers the munificence of her mother's baking, among the other preparations for Hogmanay:

My memories of Hogmanay in Kilwinning in Ayrshire are the smells of washing, baking, lavender furniture polish and Brasso. Everything had to be scrubbed, beds changed, washing and ironing done, all the rubbish put out, even the hot fire ashes carried out just before midnight. Children had to do their share of preparation on the last day of the year, getting the messages [groceries], paying the bills so that the New Year started off with a clean sheet.

My mother, like all her generation, was fanatical about her front door step being scrubbed, and the brass key plate, letterbox and bell Brasso-ed to a golden gleam. The steps were scrubbed and the edges of the steps then coated with White Cardinal and the tile window sills with Red Cardinal which replaced the donkey stone that had been used since pre-Christian times to make swirling patterns round the firestone, the hearth and the doorstep to confuse fairies and witches of ill-intent.

Dusters were recycled navy school knickers or vests. Woollen jersey remnants were used for putting on furniture polish and an old vest for buffing up the shine. Old towels or terry nappies were used for applying Brasso and Silvo to ornaments and cutlery. After polishing, the cutlery was dipped in flour and re-polished to make sure the Silvo was gone. I remember being sprawled on newspapers on the floor, relishing the shining cutlery.

Once the cleaning and washing was done it was time to start the baking. My mother baked every week, usually a girdle baking, soda and treacle scones, pancakes and Welsh Cakes. Birthdays meant a Victoria sponge or a chocolate cake and a cloutie dumpling with trinkets. The dumpling also made an appearance at Hallowe'en and New Year, but Ne'er-day also meant caraway cake, cherry cake, sultana cake, Madeira cake, gingerbread, shortbread, and the once-a-year ginger wine made with a bottle of Yulade Cordial from the Co-op mixed into boiled, cooled sweetened water; and of course Black Fadge.

When I first came across Black Bun, I thought Black Fadge was the same thing, but the only point of resemblance was the pastry case. Black Fadge was more like a gingerbread. Having treacle in it, it had to be cooked long and slow. It must be nearly fifty years since I met anyone who knew what Black Fadge was and I have never made it since I left Ayrshire.

The Black Fadge and the shortbread were the last things to be put in a cool oven. The shortbread was different from today's crisp biscuits. The butter, sugar, flour and a little ground rice or semolina were kneaded on a flat surface until it came together. The kneading made the shortbread much doughier than today's biscuits.

My mother told me that shortbread should never be cut, but only broken, and that the crimped edges were a representation of the rays of the sun. In the days when people worshipped the sun, they made its image in the middle of winter to remind it to come back. The shortbread was broken because the people gathered in amity and before the days of cutlery a knife could only be a weapon.

By the Bells, food had been laid out for first-footers. We wished each other health, wealth and happiness. The back door was opened to let the old year out and we waited for the first foot, who usually had a lump of coal and a bottle, and was expected to be a tall, dark and handsome man. A redhead, particularly a woman, was not welcome.

It was a rite of passage to be allowed to stay up 'for the Bells'. As the children became young adults, we were allowed to go first-footing, another rite of passage. No-one ever turned away a caller at their door, and at times bewildered women found themselves entertaining the odd stranger who had been absorbed by a passing crowd. I cannot remember any animosity or violent drunkenness, just general conviviality.

New Year's Day dinner was traditionally steak pie. The butchers' shelves, filled the week before with turkeys and capons, were lined with steak pies. Some ashets [large dishes] had their owner's name on them and pies made to their requirements. In some houses the meal was eaten on Hogmanay late in the evening before the Bells, but never in our house.

On New Year's Day everyone kept open house, and the neighbours who had dropped in after the bells would call by and share the hospitality, the baking and the remnants of the cloutie dumpling.

Such a home-made bounty of good things to eat may no longer be so widespread at Hogmanay. Black or Scotch Bun – the fruit-laden, pastry-encased sweetmeat whose consistency is described perfectly by George Mackay Brown as 'rich, heavy, dark, sappy' – is still easily bought from the baker's, though surely not made in many home kitchens. But the visitor who drops in on friends and neighbours at New Year is still likely to be offered some shortbread – even if it's from a packet bought at a supermarket – and a drink of some description. Robert Chambers, speaking of the early 1800s, tells of the 'het [hot] pint', a concoction of ale, whisky, sugar and nutmeg, which was carried through the streets in a large pot, in the same way that the Wassail bowl was taken around in more southerly New Year peregrinations. But for a good while now, plain whisky has been a favourite New Year drink, perhaps, in hard times, bought only once a year as a special treat. The fiery liquor's name famously derives from the Gaelic *uisge-beatha*, 'the water of life'. From 1644, increasingly heavy taxation forced its production more and more into secret stills hidden in remote places, and it's rumoured that, even today, there are still one or two secreted among the Highland heather.

Storyteller Alec Williamson has a tale which he heard in Gaelic from his father. It tells of two men who went out on a Hogmanay to look for whisky:

> There was this two fellows and they said to one another, 'We'd better get the whisky in, New Year'll not be long now.' In the Highlands then there weren't that many roads, it was mainly trails and cart tracks, so they went across a hill; probably they were going to a shebeen, where whisky was made illegally. And they came to this funny sort of knoll and one of the fellows stopped. 'Listen,' he said, 'dae ye hear that?'
>
> 'What is it?' said the other.
>
> 'It's the pipes,' he said. 'My God he can play, listen to it!'
>
> The other, well he listened a whiley, but then he said, 'Come on.' The first fellow said he'd wait a bit, so the other went to where he was going, and he got the keg, and he took it on his shoulders. He came back the way they'd taken and here was the first fellow, still on his knees, listening.
>
> 'Hey!' the second one said, 'what are you doing there?'
>
> 'Just wait a minute.'
>
> 'Ach, I canna be bothered wi' you,' said the second one and so he kept going, had a few rests and got home.
>
> Now, Hogmanay came, and the whisky, I'm sure, went out. But his companion never returned. And people got suspicious, you see, and he was arrested. He told them what happened. 'I just kept going,' he said, 'I left him where he was.' But who was going to believe him?

Nobody believed him. But there was no evidence that he'd killed him. 'He told me to come home and said he'd follow, but he never followed me.'

Well, for lack of evidence they couldn't do anything about it. A year passed and the fellow said, 'I'll be going on my own this time'. So he got across to where he got the last keg, across the hill, and to where he thought he was before. 'No,' he thought, 'not here, I'm wrong.' So he went on another bit and he heard the music again. 'That's it!' And he was there, the first fellow, on his knees.

'Are you still here?' said his companion. By that time he was needing a shave! He was in a terrible state.

'Just wait,' he said, 'till I hear the end o' this one, wait till I hear the end o' this one and I'll see yourself when you come back.'

The other went, got his whisky, back he came to the place – and he took him, by brute force, saying 'Come on!' and the man just dropped. When he came away from the knoll, and he couldna hear the music, he just died there. Aye, he died there, and the other one went home and reported it. The people knew then that it did happen, seeing the state o' him who died. And they were saying it was fairies who stole the mind o' the fellow.

And that is the story of the two men who went for the keg, and it happened on Hogmanay night.

Most families, if they had alcohol in the house at Hogmanay, would offer it to visitors more as a token of friendship than as an invitation to revelry. Some were teetotal by choice but this didn't mean that other aspects of Hogmanay celebrations weren't observed. Folk singer and songwriter Geordie McIntyre remembers:

I was born in 1937 in the district of Govanhill in south Glasgow. I was brought up in the top flat of a tenement by my grandparents and my mother, who was a single parent, and I think the nature of the family determined the type of Hogmanay and New Year's Day – Ne'er-day – we celebrated. First of all, there was no alcohol in the house, ever, when I was growing up. Now, on Hogmanay we always had cordial – ginger wine cordial or raspberry cordial – and it was the only time of the year I tasted the stuff, the only time. On that day, too, there was a special meal of steak pie, potatoes and maybe carrots and peas. I certainly remember the steak pie and potatoes; the pie was one we bought in and most certainly not what we'd eat normally.

There was at least as much concern in the past as there is today about the effects of overindulgence in alcohol at New Year, both on individuals and communities. In a pamphlet entitled *New-Year's Drinking*, issued in 1851 by The Scottish Association for Suppressing Drunkenness, the social reformer Dr Thomas Guthrie, one of the founders of the Free Church, wrote:

> The Duke of Wellington, during the Peninsular War, heard that a large magazine of wine lay on his line of march. He feared more for his men from barrels of wine than batteries of cannon, and instantly despatched a body of troops to knock every wine barrel on the head.
>
> Christmas and the New Year we fear as much. Like him, we cannot remove the temptation – shut the dram shop, and break the whiskey bottle – but we are sure that, unless you will be persuaded to avoid it, the approaching seasons will prove fatal to the life of some and the virtue of many. At no other season of the year does our town [Edinburgh] present sights so distressing and so disgusting. Well may Christians pray, and parents weep, and our churches be hung in black; there are more young men and women ruined, more bad habits contracted, and more souls lost then, than at any other season of the year.

However tragic the effects of excessive drinking might be, at New Year or at any other time, they can also be a source of great humour. Here's an anecdote that was told by the late Hamish Imlach – raconteur, folk singer and songwriter – about a Hogmanay drinking session in Glasgow:

> Stories often get taken over by different people. There's one which Billy Connolly tells as happening to him and Josh, but it was Josh [Macrae, the folk singer] and me. We went to the Clarendon Bar in St George's Road one Hogmanay afternoon. That year 31 December was a Saturday. The Clarendon was then a jazz place on weekend afternoons, and if you went in and played or sang you'd get

a double whisky on the bar. Then the landlady would shut the doors, clear the punters out, and you'd be locked in and have a session all afternoon.

I needed to get back to Motherwell, but I'd fallen out with Wilma's parents yet again, so I'd bought a cairryoot bottle to take back there, which left me without much drinking money. I'd stayed with Josh on the Friday night, and at lunchtime we went into the Clarendon, where we both did a few songs with the band, and got our double whiskies, then stayed on bevvying, with people buying us drinks.

The pub opens again at five for public business, and I think, 'No, I'd better get out and go home to Motherwell.' Josh and I lurch out, the cold evening air hits us and we learn that we are both steaming drunk. So we rest, clutching at a lamppost at St George's Cross, fifty yards away from Josh's house in Rupert Street.

Coming towards us is a wee punter, toting two big paper pokes with string handles – this was of course before the days of plastic bags. He's struggling, bunnet down over the brow, shuffling through the uncertain weather, head down against the snell wind. Suddenly one of his paper bags tears, disintegrates, and eight screw-top beer bottles hit the pavement and start to roll about. The wee punter is panicking, getting flustered, not sure which bottle to chase, and Josh and I are leaning against the lamppost looking on in horror at this dread occurrence. Then it slowly dawns on all three of us that by a miracle not one of the bottles of beer has broken.

Eight bottles are rolling about the pavement and gutter, but they are all intact. A big grin spreads over his face, we give him the thumbs up in congratulation, he bends over to pick up the first beer bottle – and a half bottle of whisky falls out of his coat pocket and smashes on the pavement. We didn't know whether to greet or go and help lap it up.

Hamish Imlach died in the early hours of 1 January 1996, peacefully, in front of the television. Not long after Hamish's death, his friend, the folk singer and broadcaster Archie Fisher, was performing at the Inverness Folk Club. He told the audience that Hamish, on the Ne'er-day morning, had been watching a programme about John Lennon, and had decided to first-foot him.

During the past couple of hundred years, newspapers have reported, often with disapproval, on the excesses of Hogmanay, even though there seem to have been few real catastrophes resulting from overindulgence. But the watchful will always be keeping an eye on our behaviour. In a contribution to *The Statistical Account of Scotland* (1793), an Edinburgh minister wrote:

In no respect was the sobriety and decorum of the lower ranks in 1763 more remarkable than by contrasting them with the riot and licentiousness of 1783, particularly on Sundays and holidays. The King's birthday, and the last night of the year were, in 1783, devoted to drunkenness, folly and riot, which in 1763 were attended with peace and harmony.

On the opposite edge of the divide, the wildness and defiance of the Daft Days, of young men out on the rant, their comradeship, the exhilaration of having been up all night, stravaiging until dawn, still standing against all the odds, with one bottle empty and two still to go, is embodied in Violet Jacob's *Hogmanay (To a Pipe Tune)*. It was published in her collection *Songs of Angus* in 1915, a year before her son died from wounds he received at the battle of the Somme:

O, it's fine when the New and the Auld Year meet,
An' the lads gang roarin' i' the lichtit street,
An' there's me and there's Alick an' the miller's loon,
An' Geordie that's the piper oot o' Forfar toon.
   Geordie Faa! Geordie Faa!
Up wi' the chanter, lad, an' gie's a blaw!
For we'll step to the tune while we've feet in till oor shune,
Tho' the bailies an' the provost be to sort us a'!

We've three bonnie bottles, but the third ane's toom,
Gin' the road ran whisky, it's mysel' wad soom!
But we'll stan' while we can, an' be dancin' while we may,
For there's twa we hae to finish, an' it's Hogmanay.
   Geordie Faa! Geordie Faa!
There's an auld carle glow'rin' oot ahint yon wa',
But we'll sune gar him loup to the pipin' till he coup,
For we'll gi'e him just a drappie, an' he'll no say na!

My heid's dementit an' my feet's the same,
When they'll no wark thegither it's a lang road hame;
An' we've twa mile to traivel or it's mair like three,
But I've got a grip o' Alick, an' ye'd best grip me.
   Geordie Faa! Geordie Faa!
The morn's near brakin' an' we'll need awa',
Gin ye're aye blawin' strang, then we'll maybe get alang,
An' the deevil tak' the laddie that's the first to fa'!

In the 1950s the way Hogmanay was celebrated began to change, as more people acquired television sets, and programmes like the New Year's edition of *The White Heather Club*, first broadcast in 1958, gave viewers an alternative to live entertainment and visiting each other's houses. Orkney storyteller and author Tom Muir was brought up on a rural farm at a time when the influence of television hadn't yet replaced some of the older ways of Hogmanay:

Anticipation was starting to build in the Muir household as Hogmanay drew nearer. As a small child in the late 1960s the approach of the New Year was a significant event, as it was the last big event to celebrate for a long, long time. Christmas was the greatest day on the festival calendar, but Hogmanay was up there in second place. Preparations had begun weeks before, as the farm where I was born started to resemble something out of a poultry horror movie, with dead hens and ducks all over the place. They were plucked in readiness for the big poultry sale at the Kirkwall Auction Mart. Many of them were destined for the tables of family and friends, and ducks were a popular meal on New Year's Day. My mother would put the duck, specially beheaded and eviscerated to keep the weight down (although still retaining its gizzard and internal organs), into a plastic bag, and wrap it in brown paper tied up with string. The package was then taken to the post office and sent through the Royal Mail to the happy recipient for their New Year's dinner.

The big thing that I looked forward to about Hogmanay was getting to stay up for the Bells at midnight. The house was filled with the smell of delicious food; our New Year's Day dinner prepared the night before by my mother. A stuffed turkey, sewn up with needle and thread to keep the stuffing in, was boiled in a pot, and a delicious soup was made from the stock. A trifle was also made in order to be properly set before morning. These things were kept in an unheated room as fridges were a rare phenomenon in Orkney at that time.

As the evening wore on, my mother's thoughts turned to entertaining any first-footers. The glass cabinet was opened and the nip glasses were set out to do their duty. They were tiny affairs, more like a modern day 'shot-glass', with a gold ring around the top and a transfer print of a pheasant on the side. Half of the glasses were filled with whisky and the other half with sweet sherry, for the ladies. Children were catered for with ginger cordial from a bottle with a white label. I never saw these bottles during the year, only at Hogmanay. The ginger cordial was sweet and fiery and I loved it. Then shortbread was set out on plates, along with black bun, or 'horse cake' as it was known in our house. Apparently it resembled some feeding supplement that was given to the work horses that pulled the agricultural machinery before the battle for the fields was lost to the tractors. The television was switched on to BBC 1 (the only channel our TV could receive) and my parents delighted in the spectacle of tartan-clad dancers skipping merrily to the sound of accordion and fiddle, while Andy Stewart, Moira Anderson and Kenneth McKellar sang upbeat Scottish ditties. If I was good (and when was I ever not good, I ask you?) I would be given a small sweet sherry to celebrate the passing of the year.

A New Year's Recipe

Recipes for traditional New Year sweetmeats, like shortbread and black bun, are easily found in books and online. But here's an unpublished version of a seasonal favourite, a cake with caraway seeds.

Elizabeth Brown runs the Highland-based home-made baking company Capability Brown's, and has a keen interest in researching Scottish culinary traditions and putting them into practice:

I still bake bannocks on the old girdle used by my Great Grannie and have one of the huge stock pots in which most cakes and puddings were boiled, over the fire, before ovens were introduced in the eighteenth century. People would have put every part of their meal in there together, some in pots, some wrapped up in muslin cloth.

Seed Cake often crops up in old recipes and can be dated back to around 1590. It was traditionally served at Hogmanay. Caraway was used a lot between the sixteenth and nineteenth centuries and the old Scots word for it was 'carvie', very similar to the French 'carvi'. The seeds were believed to have medicinal purposes, relieving a build-up of wind and easing stomach pains.

I have come across the 'Seed Cake' a lot when researching old recipes. This is my version. The mix is enough for a one pound loaf tin.

Preheat oven to 180 degrees and grease and line a 1lb. loaf tin.
6oz of butter or margarine (softened)
6oz of Demerara sugar
3 free range eggs
6oz of self-raising flour
handful of flaked almonds
handful of caraway seeds
1 tablespoon of honey (good quality heather honey works best) + a little extra for icing
1 tablespoon of whisky (good quality malt – but not too peaty) + a little extra for icing
Juice from half a lemon
About 3oz of icing sugar

Cream the fat and sugar until light and fluffy, add eggs gradually, and then fold in the rest of the ingredients apart from the lemon juice and icing sugar. Bake the cake for

approximately 35 – 40 minutes. Check after 35 minutes with a sharp knife or skewer. If it comes out clean then it's ready; if it doesn't, bake for a further 5 minutes and try again. After 10 minutes, turn out on to a wire rack to cool. While still slightly warm, prick all over with a skewer. Make up the icing using icing sugar, lemon juice, a little honey and a little whisky. Pour or drizzle over the cake, which will keep no problem for about 5 days in an airtight container. Serve when cold, with a good dram!

4

THE MAGICAL MOMENT

For many who were brought up in Scotland during or immediately after the Second World War, a vivid Hogmanay memory is of the cleaning and clearing out of the house. Lawrence Tulloch's recollections of the family house on the island of Yell in Shetland being painted and even papered are included in the earlier chapter about Yule. Geordie McIntyre, who grew up in Glasgow during the war years, recalls the house being 'completely cleaned, as clean as it could possibly be by Hogmanay', and for Alison McMorland, in Lanarkshire in the 1940s:

> ... my real early memories were the cleaning of the house for Hogmanay. We had a box bed and everything had to come from underneath that box bed to really get in there and clean it. The grate, especially, had to be cleared out and the old soot got rid of – you had to get the old soot right outside.

If there was alcohol in the house it was unlikely to be touched until after midnight – the Bells – when the windows were opened, so that the sounds of the town hall clock chiming, factory sirens, ships' hooters, and train whistles could be heard (and, in later times, the radio turned on to hear the sound of Big Ben). The back door (or the front, if the dwelling had only one entrance) might be flung open to let the Old Year out and the New Year in. Robert Chambers, in *The Book of Days* (1869), says how widespread this was in Victorian times, both in Scotland and over the border:

> One of the best known and most general of these customs is, that of sitting up till twelve o'clock on the night of the 31st December, and then, when the eventful hour has struck, proceeding to the house-door, and unbarring it

with great formality to 'let out the Old, and let in the New Year.' The evening in question is a favourite occasion for social gatherings in Scotland and the north of England, the assembled friends thus welcoming together the birth of another of Father Time's ever-increasing, though short-lived progeny. In Philadelphia, in North America, we are informed that the Old Year is there 'fired out,' and the New Year 'fired in,' by a discharge of every description of firearm – musket, fowling-piece, and pistol.

In some parts of rural Scotland firing guns at New Year still goes on, as it does in the south of England, where shots are fired into the branches of trees in the apple orchards to 'drive off the evil spirits' and ensure a good cider crop.

In the previous chapter, Janet MacInnes describes the widespread custom of 'first-footing'. Sometimes the man of the house would do the first-footing himself, to make sure there would be good fortune in the coming year, as was the case in the Glasgow household where Geordie McIntyre grew up:

There was no electricity in the house till I was 11, so there was no wireless, no Big Ben chiming midnight in the house. But that made no difference to Hogmanay, to what we called the magical moment of the Bells. It was the hooters on the Clyde, three miles away, that we listened for – the ships' hooters, you could hear them as clear as a bell. It was wonderful! My earliest memories of sound, extraneous sound, were of two things – one was the hooters on the Clyde at midnight on Hogmanay; the other was the drone of German aircraft crossing Glasgow in 1942 on their way to bomb Clydebank.

There were no songs sung on Hogmanay in the house, which was very curious as my grandfather was singing all the time, though he sang hymns, never a secular song. And we were perhaps an unusual family in another respect, in that we never had visitors at Hogmanay. What happened was, my grandfather would first-foot his own house. He would go outside the house, after the Bells – in our case the ships' hooters – and he would come in, with a piece of coal and sometimes a piece of shortbread. That was regarded as good luck, an essential ritual.

When I got into my teens and was invited beyond the house to parties, then there would be singing and there would be more cordial. And when we did visit other houses, it was always the case that if you were dark haired you were more welcome than a lighter haired person. The first person to cross the threshold, the first-footer, should ideally be male and dark haired.

The house was redd out, it was completely cleaned, as clean as it could possibly be by Hogmanay, and any rubbish taken out and downstairs. So we were bringing in the New Year with a clean house, and that had its own symbolism …

In another Glasgow tenement, Adam McNaughtan remembers folk dotting in and out – and another steak pie:

The party usually moved between three or four of the houses in the close, though folk from the other houses dropped in. Our house on the ground floor was the start of Hogmanay, seeing in the New Year for neighbours and friends. The people there had their regular party pieces, though some, like my mother and one of the first-floor neighbours who was a good light tenor, had larger repertoires. Some folk would then move off to parties elsewhere, but the majority moved upstairs to one of the other houses where a party had already begun. The final destination was always in the home of a first-floor neighbour, who was a baker by profession, for a steak-pie breakfast.

As today, many people saw in the New Year in their homes, but there was also a long-standing tradition of crowds congregating in a particular spot – high street or town square, clock steeple or market cross – to listen for the Bells, before scattering to houses far and wide. In Edinburgh, for well over a century before the focus turned to fireworks over the Castle, that place was the Tron, as the *Caledonian Mercury* reported on 2 January 1860:

The New Year was ushered in by the usual signs of welcome from a large crowd in the High Street, listening to the midnight chimes from the Tron Church which announced the end of the Old Year and the beginning of the New. And first-footing was commenced with great spirit.

In 1900, the *Inverness Courier* reported:

An immense crowd of young people assembled in the vicinity of the old Steeple on Sunday night to welcome the closing of the nineteenth century and, when the clock struck the hour of midnight, loud cheers were raised and pistols and toy cannons were fired. After midnight, first-footing expeditions were as numerous as usual and singing and concertina-playing were indulged on a large scale.

And two accounts from the small Angus town of Brechin, 100 years apart, could be almost interchangeable. On 3 January 1862, the *Dundee, Perth and Cupar Advertiser* reported:

Scarcely had the last breath of the old year been allowed to depart, ere a motley throng gave vent to three cheers on the High Street, where also the Rifle Band assembled and played several airs. A general rush was then made to go first-footing.

Now Lindsey Payne's recollections from the late 1950s and early '60s:

… a crowd of us girls from school would go down to the Market Cross in Brechin, and we'd bring in the New Year there. People would be passing round bottles and then we'd go first-footing. We'd end up in people's houses that I didn't know at all, but you were sort of carried along with it! And it was all, 'Come in, sit down, have a drink!' and, 'How's your father, and what are you doing now?' And you'd get home at about five or six in the morning.

While in Kenmore, in rural Perthshire, again in the 1950s and '60s, Vonne Hammerstone remembers people gathering in the hotel:

… which was a kind of fishing hotel and our local, just before midnight, and they would give everybody in the village a drink, to bring in the New Year. At midnight the hotel would put the radio on, for Big Ben, and everybody would sing *Auld Lang Syne*. But then people would go to each other's houses. Somebody might say 'Geordie's first!' – so Geordie and Elma would bash off down the road quickly so they'd be ready to welcome everybody in, and they made sure that somebody tall and dark first-footed them – brought in black bun and whisky and fuel, usually coal in those days. And then you'd go from house to house – there were only about a hundred people all together, it was quite a small village – everybody would go round one another's houses. Beforehand, people would bake a lot of stuff, ready for everyone coming. So, as you went round the houses there was always plenty to eat, drink was provided and you took drink with you as well. And my Mum, and I think many others too, made sure you had a good meal before you went out. Her tradition was steak and kidney pie, we always had that on Hogmanay. When we were teenagers we might split off – the parents to one house and us to another – so basically there were all these parties going on in different parts of the village. Goodness knows what time we got to bed; most folk stayed up all night. It was very nice, mostly very, very good natured and everyone knew everyone else. It was fun!

Arthur Dutch, tinsmith and raconteur, who was brought up in Stockbridge in Edinburgh, has first memories of Hogmanay just after the end of the Second World War:

The very first New Year I can remember clearly was on the cusp of 1945 and '46 and I'll tell you why that was – well, I was nine, and my parents must have decided that I was old enough to stay up and enjoy New Year. But it was also the first New Year that the gas lamps had been on in the street, the first time after the war.

My sister and I were allowed to stay up and we brought New Year in, in our own house – we stayed at number 12 and my Grannie and Granddad Dutch stayed at number 10, so we left our hoose to go up and first-foot them. My father had his half bottle but I had two wee paper parcels with bits o' coal in them, one for each o' ma grannies. Anyway, we went up the next stair and wished them a Happy New Year. And Grannie had a Dover Stove and a crooked thing to lift up the flap – and I would put this wee bit paper wi' the coal into the stove – that was what I was told to do. And then, my Grannie had this thing – that you had to eat something and you had to get a drink – and the drink was ginger wine, I can taste it yet. And she used to make her shortbread in rounds, about the size of a supper plate, and she used to wrap it in a clean tea-towel; and I thought it was a great honour – she used to break it by hitting you on the head with it! And then you got a bit of the shortbread and that was that. And you wished each other a Happy New Year and there might have been a neighbour come in at the same time.

But then we left that hoose and walked to my other Grannie's and that was maybe a fifteen or twenty minute walk along the road. And it was the same process, the wee bit paper with the coal in it, throw it on the fire and wish them Happy New Year. But you just spent a few minutes there; there was quite a lot o' folk there because by that time the War had ended and she'd had two or three laddies, sons-in-law and so on, at the War and they'd started to come hame. So that house was mair crowded than the previous Grannie's house. And then you walked hame.

More than 100 years previously, first-footing in Edinburgh suddenly declined for a time. Robert Chambers (1867) explains what happened:

Till very few years ago in Scotland, the custom of the wassail bowl at the passing away of the old year might be said to be still in comparative vigour. On the approach of twelve o'clock, a *hot pint* was prepared – that is, a kettle or flagon full of warm, spiced, and sweetened ale, with an infusion of spirits. When the clock had struck the knell of the departed year, each member of the family drank of this mixture 'A good health and a happy New Year and many of them' to all the rest, with a general hand-shaking, and perhaps a dance round the table, with the addition of a song to the tune of *Hey tuttie taitie*:

'Weel may we a' be,
Ill may we never see,
Here's to the king
And the gude companie! ...'

The elders of the family would then most probably sally out, with the hot kettle, and bearing also a competent provision of buns and short-bread, or bread and cheese, with the design of visiting their neighbours, and interchanging with them the same cordial greetings. If they met by the way another party similarly bent, whom they knew, they would stop and give and take sips from their respective kettles. Reaching the friend's house, they would enter with vociferous good wishes, and soon send the kettle a-circulating. If they were the first to enter the house since twelve o'clock, they were deemed as

the *first-foot*; and, as such, it was most important, for luck to the family in the coming year, that they should make their entry, not empty-handed, but with their hands full of cakes and bread and cheese; of which, on the other hand, civility demanded that each individual in the house should partake.

To such an extent did this custom prevail in Edinburgh in the recollection of persons still living, that, according to their account, the principal streets were more thronged between twelve and one in the morning than they usually were at midday. Much innocent mirth prevailed, and mutual good feelings were largely promoted. An unlucky circumstance, which took place on the 1st January of 1812, proved the means of nearly extinguishing the custom. A small party of reckless boys formed the design of turning the innocent festivities of *first-footing* to account for purposes of plunder. They kept their counsel well. No sooner had the people come abroad on the principal thoroughfares of the Old Town, than these youths sallied out in small bands, and commenced the business which they had undertaken. Their previous agreement was, to *look out for the white neckcloths*, such being the best mark by which they could distinguish in the dark individuals likely to carry any property worthy of being taken. A great number of gentlemen were thus spoiled of their watches and other valuables. The least resistance was resented by the most brutal maltreatment. A policeman, and a young man of the rank of a clerk in Leith, died of the injuries they had received. An affair so singular, so uncharacteristic of the people among whom it happened, produced a widespread and lasting feeling of surprise. The outrage was expiated by the execution of three of the youthful rioters on the chief scene of their wickedness; but from that time, it was observed that the old custom of going about with the hot pint – the ancient wassail – fell off.

There are many reasons why seasonal celebrations and customs begin to wane, and sometimes die away: wars, when young men are forced to leave small communities, can cause at least a hiatus; religious or civil proscription can deter all but the most determined or foolhardy from continuing in their practice; some customs just run out of steam. And sometimes quite unpredictable factors can have a devastating effect. In Orkney, and other rural areas, the drink-driving laws altered New Year visiting for ever, as Tom Muir recalls:

Living in the country your next-door neighbour could be half a mile or more away and they used to come along for a visit by torchlight. Driving from house to house was once the norm, but this stopped in Orkney due to two people; Barbara Castle and David Barrogill Keith. Barbara Castle, the Labour Minister for Transport, had introduced the breathalyser in 1967, which had put some off driving from party to party (but not many in the early days). It seems incredible now that lawyers once actually used the excuse 'My client has little recollection of the accident as he was drunk at the time' in a court of law. The second reason was Sheriff D. B. Keith, a man of inconsistent judgement who took a dim view of motoring offences, the bread and butter of the Orkney constabulary. Legend has it that the sentence you could expect from Sheriff Keith was entirely dependent on the quality of his breakfast that morning (there was even a poem written about it). If the breakfast was of a high quality, with toast and eggs just the way he liked them, then you could expect a fine of a few bob and a short ticking off. But, on the other hand, should the toast be burnt and the eggs overdone, then a person facing the same charge as the previous miscreant could have the book thrown at them with considerable vigour. With a distinct lack of murders, armed robberies and arson attacks in Orkney, drunk driving was usually the worst crime to come before the Sheriff, and could be dealt with in a ruthless manner (unless the breakfast that morning had been particularly fine).

On the other hand, those people who could not afford a car were seldom the worse for wear from drink; it was poured out sparingly and there was a long and often cold walk ahead from house to house. The whisky was also soaked up by generous helpings of shortbread and horse cake too. Hogmanay was a gentle, good-natured affair with laughter, song and stories by the fireside and it seemed to have a lot more meaning in those days than it does now.

The great Highland storyteller Ailig Iain MacUilleim – Alec John Williamson – was born into a Traveller family in Rheguile, a little hilltop community above Edderton in Ross-shire, '1932, the last day of December, Hogmanay night. My Granny was the midwife, gave me a skelp on the bum, and I took to the bottle right away!'

In Alec's youth the Highland Travellers would spend the winter months in a settled place and take to the road in the spring. They travelled by horse and cart, lived in tents, and made their living tinsmithing, horse-dealing, hawking, pearl-fishing and labouring for the farmers. It was during the winter, around the hearth at Garden Cottage, the house his father had built in Rheguile, that Alec heard – in Gaelic – most of the stories he tells today. Here is his account of Hogmanays and first-footing in the Edderton area in the 1940s:

In the house, at Rheguile, you waited till 12 before you'd take any alcohol. When I'd grown up, myself and my brother would be just after coming back from Tain [the nearest town]. My father would have been into town during the day but we always went at night and, och, we'd have a few drinks in Tain and we bought what we were going to buy and came back. And then nothing until 12 o'clock. But when the clock chimed, everybody would get up and wish everyone a Happy New Year and drams would go out then. And maybe a first-footer would come in. He'd have a bit of coal, a piece of bread, and maybe a drink as well, and he put it on the table. A bit of coal so your house would never be without heat, a bit of bread so your house would never be without food …

Oh and then I went visiting. In those days, you know, the parish was split over Hogmanay and the New Year, because the people that lived in the big metropolis of Edderton village and up the Rheguile road, they were Church of Scotland, and they held it on the 1st of January. But the people away out on the crofts and beyond there up to the Struie road, they held it on the 12th of January, you see. They were all Free Church. I didn't bother with the village at all, I took the road away up.

There was one character, Big Jess we called her. She lived on a good croft, herself and her sister. Her sister was married at one time and her name was Mrs Marshall, but her man must have died and so she came back to stay. And they had a brother who went across to China and he had a few plantations out there, tea plantations; and I think he was also in what they called then Ceylon – Sri Lanka they call it today. He had plantations there too and he was well off. Now they had money to start off with; the old man had money and they had a nice house. The brother, out in the Orient, he would

be sending a lot of stuff to them, and he'd be sending them money, especially when it was coming near to Christmas, and he knew that on the 12th of January they'd be having the big Hogmanay. And he'd be sending them goodies and whisky and what not, and money. So they were in, this one Hogmanay, Mrs Marshall and Big Jess, and somebody came in – he came in and Jess said to her sister, 'Put out a dram, sister.' The dram was put out, they gave one to the stranger and to the two of themselves. Well, they said, 'A good New Year to you, sister.' And again, 'A good New Year to you, sister.' And then, 'God Bless Shanghai!'

That was one o' the stories about Jess. She was a great character, tall as the Empire State Building you know. And she dressed in this Victorian rig-out – the skirt would be so long it would be sweeping the land behind her – and she had a hat wi' a big pin in it, through the hair to keep the hat on; boots laced away up to the knees. A real old-fashioned woman, you know.

I heard this story – I knew the man it happened to, a very, very nice man. He was a cobbler, called Donald Ross; his house is still up and there's folk in it today. He was called Donald Forty – there was that many Donald Rosses in the parish school, in the primary, that they had to number them randomly. There was Donald Ross 20, Donald Ross 30 or 40 or 50 – but he was the only one that kept it. The family was known as the Forties.

Now, I'll tell ye. A Hogmanay night he came home from Tain. Oh this is many, many years ago, before my time. Anyway, he had a girlfriend and her name was MacLennan, Mary MacLennan. He had a good shot o' drink on him, you know, and he thought, 'Och I'll go up and propose tonight.' He came to the door, knocked on the door and a woman came to the door. 'Oh hello,' he said, 'I came up to go down on one knee.'

'Oh,' she said, 'I don't think you can even stay on yer feet.'

But anyway, down he went. 'Will you marry me, make me the happiest man in the parish?'

'I will,' she said. And it was the sister! He was that drunk that he took her for the girlfriend! Well, do you know, that two they got married – she kept him to his word, the sister did. And those two women never spoke to one another as long as they were alive. And the shoemaker, whether he was happy, God knows – but that's what happened on a Hogmanay night.

There were a lot o' stories in Edderton on Hogmanay night and there were a lot o' characters in Edderton, as I've many a time said. They all liked a dram, whether it was Hogmanay or not. They'd go to Tain and maybe two or three o' them would take a bottle and then they'd go to the stone called

'Clach an Dram', the dram stone, and there's where they'd have a dram. And then they'd come home and go to each other's houses, or anywhere, and of course they'd get more drams there.

There was other folk you would visit. There was this fellow called the Eigheachd. He stayed on the hill at Edderton and you'd know his house from any o' them 'cause the smoke would be coming through every vent except the chimney! He was making good money cutting and selling peat.

There was another cratur, Teenie Lachie. She wasn't as big as Big Jess but she wore the same sort o' clothes. I mind o' her. She had a brother, Davie, and Davie lived in one end o' the house and she lived in the other. They never got on, ye see, they always quarrelled. The Lachies they called them.

And I remember the Culs: Ali the Cul, Kate the Cul, Belle the Cul – another name in Gaelic for a nook or a corner.

Now all these people, every one o' them, was Free Church. They kept the Old New Year, as they called it, it was the 12th. The rest o' them, the Church of Scotland, they said it was the 1st. We kept the 1st. But many a time I heard my father – he'd be talking about weather or something – and he'd say,

'Oh it was between the two New Years,' and you'd know exactly what he meant. You'll not hear those kind o' words today, but many a time I heard him say, 'between the two New Years'.

Visiting the houses went on for hours. The last house that I would call at was the MacPhersons – Jimmy MacPherson and his wife Bessie – I'd call in there. It was a good night wi' them, there'd be a few in there. People would be dancing, dancing about – playing mooth organs, playing the fiddle, playing the pipes sometimes; there was always a musician in every house. Then a story, a joke, and a song – great, great Hogmanays.

5

FIRE AND FROLICS

In damp and chilly northern climes, warmth is so essential to human survival, and light such a potent force in staving off winter gloom, that it's not surprising to find fire and hearth central to the things that people once did, and still do, to celebrate Hogmanay. In Scotland 300 years and more ago fire was central to celebrations at four particular times of the year. In early May there were the Beltane bonfires, often accompanied by a feast. At Midsummer, after sunset, people lit fires in front of their houses; there were street parties with food and drink, and sunwise circuits of crops were made with burning torches. At Hallowe'en – the Celtic *Samhain* – up to the nineteenth century, there were yet more illumined processions round the fields, people would welcome envelopment by the bonfire smoke, and sometimes the effigies of witches were burnt in the flames. And during the Yule season, from before Christmas until well into January, flaming brands, and later burning half-barrels, were carried in celebrations that, in the fishing communities of North East Scotland, were closely associated with the boats in the harbour.

Though the spring and summer fires no longer burn, Guy Fawkes Night is widely celebrated on 5 November, somewhere between New and Old Hallowe'en, and – widespread throughout Scotland – the flames from torches, blazing barrels, bonfires and fireballs still light up midwinter evenings. Much of what we know about these fire customs in earlier times comes from ecclesiastical records kept at a time when the Reformed Church was determined to eradicate practices which smacked of Catholicism or pagan superstition. For example, in June 1655, the Dingwall Presbytery passed a resolution warning congregation members who might be considering celebrating Midsummer to 'desist from the superstitious abuses used on St John's Day by burning torches through their cornes and fires in their towns …' On 20 January 1689, the parish records of Duffus in Moray cite a young man from Burghead for having made 'a burning clavie, paying a superstitious worship and blessing the boats after the old heathenish custom'; and, on 3 February, Alexander Farquhar confessed that he 'did carry meat and drink to the boat side and did cast drink upon the boat', and John Farquhar and Elspet Young were both named as accomplices in this scandalous act of libation. It's not clear exactly what was meant here by the word 'clavie', and in some cases it was certainly used to mean a flaming torch, but by the latter half of the nineteenth century the Burghead Clavie was known and celebrated widely as a blazing tar barrel, which was carried round the streets of the small town every year (Sundays excepted) on 11 January – Old New Year's Eve. Burghead is eight miles north-west of Elgin, situated on a spit of land that juts out into the southern reaches of the Moray Firth. Though the present town was laid out in the early 1800s, its history is much older, as it encompasses an Iron Age fort where six renowned stone slabs, carved with bulls in the Pictish style, were uncovered during excavations.

In his *Book of Days* (1869), Robert Chambers quotes from the *Banffshire Journal* a vivid and lengthy account of Clavie Night, which suggests similar motives to those recorded in the seventeenth century, with the Clavie being 'carried in triumph round every vessel in the harbour, and a handful of grain thrown into each, in order to insure success for the coming year'. Though the *Journal* correspondent says that this was no longer happening, there is a later instance of the Clavie visiting a single ship – together with the sprinkling of grain – recorded as late as 1875 (though it's said that the vessel sank, putting an end to that aspect of the ceremony once and for all).

The Clavie became a celebrated custom which was, and still is, reported annually in local and national papers and magazines. Here is a less well-known account from a 1907 newspaper clipping:

> The little fishing village of Burghead, on the Moray Firth, is not generally classed among the show places of the British Isles, but on Friday they had a show which was absolutely unique.
>
> It is surprising to see an apparently law-abiding and God-fearing community given over to the rites of pagan worship, yet that is exactly what happens for the space of a couple of hours or so every year when the residents indulge in the ceremony of Burning the Clavie.

Friday was New Year's Eve according to the old calendar, and on every Old New Year's Eve the inhabitants of Burghead forget all about business, lay down their nets, give fish a rest for the day, and let themselves go, for Old New Year's Eve is the day when one burns the clavie. For the benefit of those who do not know what a clavie is, and are unversed in the ways of burning them, I would explain that the clavie is a sacred flare or beacon, which is carried round the town of Burghead once a year to render the town free from witches, and to make it prosperous for the coming year.

The clavie, as befits an instrument dedicated to a sacred cause, is not just any old sort of bonfire. On the contrary, the manufacture of it is both skilled and artistic. The committee that sits over the construction of the clavie is a very exclusive body of men known as the clavie crew. They number four, including the real head of the undertaking, who is called the clavie skipper, or the clavie king.

This personage is Mr William Peterkin. He has been clavie skipper for almost forty years, and probably knows more about the business of clavie burning than any man living. His father was skipper before him.

A REAL BEAUTY

The clavie is a barrel, or to be more accurate, half a barrel. It is one of the unofficial duties of the Provost of Burghead to provide a barrel for the year's clavie.

The present Provost (Mr George D. Gordon) hunted in the back of his shop and produced a real beauty well worthy to be made into a clavie.

At three o'clock in the afternoon the barrel is taken to the appointed place, and there the crew set to work upon it. Previous to that, they are not supposed to have seen the barrel, as that brings bad luck.

First of all, the barrel has to be sawn in two; it is then ready for the handle to be fixed. The lower half of the barrel is fixed on to a wooden shaft by means of a special nail, provided for the purpose by the blacksmith. The nail is thrust home by blows with a heavy stone, as it is most important that no hammer be used in the construction of the clavie, for this would render its charms powerless.

When the handle is fixed firmly the clavie is filled full of peat, dry wood, and anything that will burn. All is then liberally soaked in tar, so that it forms a very combustible torch.

The clavie is now complete. The whole village waits for darkness to fall.

At six o'clock bus loads of people have arrived from all parts of the district, and presently the show begins.

The brawny crew get under the clavie and this is lighted by means of a lump of burning peat; it would be sacrilege to light the clavie with a match, as these are as unlucky as hammers.

When the torch is well ablaze the crew move off, and the burning of the clavie has begun. How those four brawny men are able to carry that blazing, spluttering, roaring mass without being roasted I do not know.

The burning mass is continually dripping boiling tar and crackling cinders over their backs and arms and giving an impressive firework display as it goes along, but the crew seem made of brass.

IN AT THE OPEN DOOR

The bearers have now to carry the clavie all through the town, and they move off, carried by a large and hilarious crowd, and outside every important door they stop and throw a piece of the burning clavie through the open door, as the possession of a clavie faggot brings a year's luck. As was only fitting, the Provost got the first and largest lump. His clavie was really an incandescent mass of burning wood and peat which when hurled through his door had sufficient power to set the whole house on fire.

The procession keeps on winding in and out the little streets, and all the small boys fight for the pieces as they drop off the clavie.

Nobody cares for burnt fingers now, although when I tried to get an excellent piece I dropped it quicker than I had picked it up. However I bought a piece for two-pence from a small boy who had an armful, so my luck is assured.

Every now and again the crew would stop and fling a bit of the blazing stuff through somebody's door. They just picked it off the clavie with their bare fingers which undoubtedly were not flesh and blood.

I heard that pieces of the clavie are sent to Burghead folk abroad, which isn't fair, as they didn't have to get their fingers burnt.

Gradually, and with many stoppages, the clavie makes a circuit of the town, and is brought finally to its ultimate goal, the Doorie Hill. This is a little knob of land at the east end of the town and is specially dedicated to the use of the clavie.

At the top of the Doorie Hill is a sort of cairn of stones cemented into a little tower. This is called the Clavie Pillar, and was presented to the clavie by a late Provost.

Up here the clavie, still blazing merrily, is carried, and the handle is placed in a socket in the top of the pillar.

The clavie's journey is now at an end, and the real fire worship begins. More fuel is heaped upon the huge torch, a new bucket of tar poured over its dripping sides, and the flames shoot up into the sky a beacon for miles around. The other half of the Provost's barrel is produced, and is smashed down on top of the clavie. Very soon that blazes up as well, and the crowd of watchers on the top, sides, and bottom of the Doorie Hill shriek with excitement.

AN IMPRESSIVE SIGHT

It is not as childish as it sounds. The blazing clavie topping the stone pillar, illuminating the faces below with a lurid glow is a very impressive sight. I shouted as loudly as anybody there. More fuel! More tar on the clavie! More shrieks from the watchers!

The clavie crew, Salamander-like, pass in and out of the flames tossing spare lumps of wood to those below.

Then, for some unaccountable reason, the clavie roars and splits, hundreds of flaring faggots sail into the air scattering all but the crew. The force of the explosion makes the flames whistle in the air.

There is a mighty rush for the lumps of fuel which are rolling down the hill. Some little boys get an armful! Some beefy fishermen don't get any! Nobody minds! The clavie itself being only wood and tar, at last it begins to subside, the flames grow less and less, but not until there is nothing left but smouldering ashes do people leave to catch the last bus home.

In the morning the Doorie Hill is littered with faggots black and cold, and the little fishing village of Burghead on the Moray Firth is free from witches for another year.

The anonymous writer, 'A Special Correspondent', artfully slips from a tone which is affectionately tongue-in-cheek to one of being completely carried along, physically and emotionally, by the procession of the blazing tar barrel and its followers through the maze of the streets to the climax on the Doorie Hill. It is an account which, with very few changes, could be a vivid description of Old New Year's night in Burghead over 100 years later. Today a police presence which increases annually in numbers reflects contemporary concerns for Health and Safety, rather than the anticipation of any disorderly behaviour. In the past, things could be much wilder. In an interview recorded in 1986, Dan Ralph, who is the present Clavie King, recalls when the young people of Burghead would hold their own Clavie at the modern Hogmanay, using small herring barrels:

> ... as opposed to the big barrels. The youngsters of the town carried them around burning them – wandering the streets – no particular route. I can remember being about five or six when it happened the last time. They all gathered, six or seven of them, in the middle of the street up at the Post Office corner and they dumped the whole lot in the middle. Of course the tar melted; the overhead wires came down; doors were burned; windows were cracked. I think about a dozen of them were arrested. Jailed in Elgin ... It had been a long standing tradition as well. I think it was the youngsters' way of proving themselves, that they could also be in the Clavie crew when they were big enough.

In Victorian times, tar barrel processions were popular and widespread, and there may well have been a fashion for them. In 1913, a correspondent in the *Campbeltown Courier* describes

Hogmanay night revelries in the 1860s, very like today's New Year tar barrels in Allendale, Northumberland:

> Down the street came a procession of tar barrels full ablaze, followed by hundreds of townspeople, all wending their way to the Cross. The flaming barrels were carried on the heads of five picked men, and attendants marched on either side battering at the staves with sticks to increase the flame of the fire. Continuous cheers were shouted from every throat. The windows of the houses along the route were all open, with the occupants leaning out to witness the scene …

In *The Graphic* – a weekly illustrated newspaper – for 7 January 1893, in a column entitled 'Galloway New Year Customs', Miss E.M. Johnstone writes that among the customs in Newton Stewart:

> … the grand sight of all, and the climax, is the procession of young men which parades the village on New Year's Eve … every one vies with the other as to which shall present the most bizarre appearance. Red Indians, giants, dwarfs, demons (assorted and of all sizes) and fishwives pass in procession, carrying at intervals flaming tar-barrels, and finally gathering in a wild dance round a flaming bonfire, for which all the neighbouring woods have been laid under contribution.

In the latter half of the nineteenth century blazing tar barrels were also an important feature of midwinter celebrations in Shetland. In *Shetland: Descriptive and Historical and Topographical Description of that Country* (1879), Robert Cowie, himself a Shetlander, writes:

The Christmas season, which has always been held with more than ordinary merriment in Scandinavia, is still kept in the good old Norse fashion by the Lerwegians. With the outset of winter, the ingenuous youths of Lerwick commence preparation for Yule, taking care to observe the strictest secrecy. On Christmas Eve, the 4th January – for the old style is still observed – the children go *a guizing*, that is to say, disguising themselves in the most fantastic and gaudy costumes, they parade the streets, and infest the houses and shops, begging for the wherewithal to carry on their Christmas amusements. One o'clock on Yule morning having struck, the young men turn out in large numbers, dressed in the coarsest of garments, and, at the double-quick march, drag huge tar barrels through the town, shouting and cheering as they go, or blowing loud blasts with their 'louder horns.' The tar barrel simply consists of several – say from four to eight – tubs filled with tar and chips, placed on a platform of wood. It is dragged by means of a chain, to which scores of jubilant youths readily yoke themselves. They have recently been described by the burgh officer of Lerwick as 'fiery chariots, the effect of which is truly grand and terrific.' In a Christmas morning the dark streets of Lerwick are generally lighted up by the bright glare, and its atmosphere blackened by the dense smoke, of six or eight tar barrels in succession. On the appearance of daybreak, at six A.M., the morning revellers put off their coarse garments – well begrimed by this time – and in turn become guizards. They assume every imaginable form of costume – those of soldiers, sailors, Highlanders, Spanish Chevaliers, &c. Thus disguised, they either go in pairs, as man and wife, or in larger groups, and proceed to call on their friends, to wish them the compliments of the season. Formerly, these adolescent guizards used to seat themselves in crates, and accompanied by fiddlers, were dragged through the town. The crate, however, has for some years fallen into disuse. After the revels of the morning, they generally grow pretty languid ere evening arrives. Old New Year's Day (12th January), is kept similarly to Christmas, but the rejoicings it calls forth are usually on a smaller scale.

Lerwick wasn't the only place where a crate was hauled around as part of midwinter celebrations. In 1927, a correspondent wrote to the *Glasgow Herald*, recalling, some sixty years before, the 'Burning of the Crate' in Dingwall, Ross-shire:

> ... the burning of the crate was carried out by the youth of the town. For some weeks before Hogmanay, about twenty of the more adventurous young spirits of the time built a hut secreted in a neighbouring wood, where they prepared for the Day, or rather, the Night. First, an old horse (termed a 'nag') was bought from travelling tinkers for a few shillings. It was tethered at the hut and fed with the best of corn and hay, begged or otherwise procured from farmers in the vicinity. A large crate was purchased from a crockery dealer in the town and duly filled with combustibles well-soaked with paraffin.
>
> This was jealously guarded for the three weeks during which the musicians of the party practised on various instruments – principally home-made whistles, triangles of wire, tambourines, and drums made from tin boxes – for the 'band' which was to escort the procession from the hut into the town on the night before January 1.
>
> The procession consisted of the band, followed by the nag pulling the crate, the crate being surrounded by half a dozen of the youths fantastically dressed, the horse being ridden by another youth, the leader, dressed as a Red Indian in full flow of feather and paint. When the procession entered the High Street, the contents of the crate were fired and the burning mass was dragged by the horse towards the Cross at the front of the Municipal Buildings, the processionists meanwhile engaging in a riot of whooping and dancing, winding up the orgy by scattering the flaming contents of the crate when the town clock sounded the first stroke of twelve. The 'jazz' band (long before the modern jazz was heard of) then struck up the popular New Year tunes of the period and the proceedings ended in a general melee of song and handshaking.
>
> Latterly the crate-burning became a danger to property (many wooden houses then existing on the High Street) and the police had to interfere. Without the burning crate the

procession lost its attraction and eventually the nag, the crate and the band became a thing of the past.

Just as the police put an end to the Dingwall crate celebrations, the same fate might have befallen the Lerwick tar barrels, but instead, beginning in the 1870s, they started to become organised into the celebration which today is called 'Up Helly Aa'', held in Lerwick on the last Tuesday in January, which proclaims itself to be 'Europe's Largest Fire Festival'. Although Up Helly Aa attracts visitors from all over the world, it's essentially a local celebration, a day that culminates with a torchlight procession of forty-five guizer squads led by the Jarl squad – men who are decked out in fantastical Viking costumes – and their chief, the Guizer Jarl, leading to the burning of a replica Viking galley. After the conflagration, the crowd disperses to the twelve halls throughout the town, where food is laid on and dancing is interspersed with visits from the different guizer squads. The men who make up the squads – up to a couple of dozen in each – are costumed as topical characters, such as Osama Bin Laden, or cross-dressed, and perform turns they have rehearsed specially (and preparations for Up Helly Aa go on throughout the whole of the previous year). The celebrations can last until 6 a.m. the following morning, and visitors are warned that they will need plenty of stamina to see the night through.

The custom of processing with flaming torches, like the clavies that were taken round the fields and boats in seventeenth-century Moray, is still embodied in the Comrie Flambeaux. At midnight on Hogmanay evening, eight or more flambeaux are lit and paraded through the streets of the Perthshire village, with a pipe band in attendance, before they are tossed into the waters of the River Earn, to the roars of the crowd. The torches, which tower above the heads of the carriers, are made from saplings, wrapped in sacking, which have been soaked in paraffin for three weeks before they are lit. There's no record that the custom has a long history, though there is a local tradition that, in earlier times, stags' heads were paraded round the village, and Comrie folk are happy to speak of a pagan origin.

Another Hogmanay event which attracts great crowds is the bonfire in the Lanarkshire town of Biggar, where a massive blaze is kindled in the middle of the high street. In the past, the infrequent objection raised by a newly resident incomer has been neatly parried. On one occasion in the 1990s, a compromise was reached with an agreement that the Fire Brigade would dowse the flames at half past midnight; but, after this was accomplished and the firemen had returned to their station, the bonfire was reignited with 'thirty gallons of diesel' which had been put by especially for the purpose. The spirit of the Biggar bonfire was kept alive during the black-out of the Second World War, when, says Marion McNeill, 'a housewife whose door was a few yards from the bonfire site regularly went out ... on the stroke of twelve and welcomed in the New Year with the flame of a match!'

The North East fishing port of Stonehaven, on the coast to the south of Aberdeen, is celebrated for its annual Hogmanay Fireballs procession, where forty or more blazing balls made from chicken wire packed with paraffin-soaked combustibles such as newspaper, coal, kindling and rags are swung around the heads of their kilted bearers as they parade through the streets. While there's no historical evidence for the Fireballs, as they exist today, going back much more than a century, their enormous success as a public event, drawing up to 10,000 spectators, shows how potent is the attraction of midwinter fire. On 10 January 1930, the *Mearns Leader* carried an account of the Fireballs from a Mr George D. Banks, which tells of a town transformed by the exuberance and conviviality of the midwinter fire celebrations:

'Ye maunna miss the fireballs, A'body gings tae see them', I recalled my landlady's words as I mingled with the waiting crowd in the old High Street. Everybody evidently was there.

It was Sauchiehall Street on a four-foot pavement, but, with one big difference. Here, the spirit of friendship prevailed. A more jovial throng than this one would be hard put to find, even if the exploding fireworks failed to upset its equanimity. Everyone was happy; each one knew the other, except my self. I, a stranger in a strange town, separated from home by business, knew no one and was known to none.

As the clock pointed to the hour, the bell pealed out and a murmur rippled up the street, 'A Happy New Year' echoed from mouth to mouth. I felt the truth of the saying that a man can be loneliest in a crowd.

An old fisherman beside me held out his hand, 'I dinna ken ye bit I wish ye a Happy New Year'. I grabbed his hand heartily. I was struck with the singularity of the situation. Here was I passing the first minutes of the New Year in an old street with old houses, in the company of an old man.

Just then the houses near The Cross were lit up with a ruddy glare. The sight was wonderful – what might have been an army of demons issuing from their fiery den. First one swaying figure, whirling a great fire-ball, appeared, silhouetted against the glare, then another, and another advanced up the street, till the scene lost its reality. It became more like a nightmare, the creation of a fanciful mind.

The thick clouds of smoke and the myriad of sparks, the masses of blazing debris on the roadway and the figures appearing and disappearing in what seemed a solid mass of fire, were like beings in torment. It was like a scene from Dante's Inferno.

Recovering from my first astonishment at the scene, I turned to greet the old fisherman, but, like the proverbial good fairy, he had disappeared. I was determined to follow

this excellent example, and, approaching a group nearby, I repeated the fisherman's formula. They responded with the right spirit, as did everyone I spoke to. I changed my opinion of the people of Stonehaven. Hitherto I had thought them stiff and formal. Now I will always think of them as cheery good-natured people.

At last when the last fireball had burnt itself out, and the last swinger had staggered away into the darkness, the old gables began to lose their glamour and to sink into their everyday drabness. I joined the dispersing crowd, they to their first-footing and I – to bed.

6

STRANGE VISITORS

When Hogmanay and midwinter celebrations were in their heyday, it was expected that neighbours and relatives would first-foot and call round with drams and gifts of food; but many households could also expect a visit from the Guisers. In earlier times they would be adults – both men and women – though by the nineteenth century, they were increasingly likely to be a band of young people or children who could invade your home without even knocking at the door, sweep the floor, sing songs, perform a play, or just create a bit of mayhem, and then leave, sometimes with a few coppers, but generally having eaten or collected food which you had specially prepared for the occasion: 'bread and cheese, currant loaf, hogmanays (or three-cornered biscuits) and, in some houses, whisky to those who were more grown up'.

A distinguishing feature of the Guisers, as their name suggests, is that they hid their identities. Most simply this might mean blacking some of the face with soot or burnt cork, or, as in the early decades of the twentieth century, buying penny masks from the local store. But it could entail something much more elaborate, as in Thomas Edmondston's description of Shetland Yule celebrations from the late 1860s:

> The straw suits are still, in some parts of the Shetland Islands, worn by the peasantry in order to disguise themselves when going from house to house at Hallowmas or Martinmas, and at Christmas. Those disguised are sometimes termed, as in Scotland, 'gyzarts' and also in some localities 'skeklers,' but I have not ascertained the meaning of the latter term. The straw helmet is usually ornamented with long streamers of ribbons of different colours. One of the pieces surrounds the neck and

covers the shoulders, the larger covers the middle and
the narrow bits are anklets. The face is covered partially
with a coloured handkerchief. The maskers go from
house to house, and if possible accompanied by a fiddler,
performing the most grotesque dances, expecting a dram
or small gratuity. The custom is fast dying out; it is not
easy to procure a complete suit.

A photograph from 1909 of boys dressed as Skeklers shows their
bodies entirely covered by the three-piece straw costume (though
their faces are revealed, presumably for the photograph). Perhaps
coincidentally they closely resemble the Irish Christmas mummers
– the Straw Boys – whose high, conical hats cover their faces
entirely. In *Popular Rhymes of Scotland* (1841), the indefatigable
Robert Chambers describes Guisers, perhaps as he saw them when
he was a boy in Peebles a couple of decades earlier (the sweeping
of the house, mentioned in his account, was not restricted to
Scotland; in the Yorkshire Pennines at New Year the 'mummers'
would enter houses disguised, sweeping the floor and humming as
they went about their labours):

The doings of the *guizards* (that is, masquers) form
a conspicuous feature in the New-year proceedings
throughout Scotland. The evenings on which these
personages are understood to be privileged to appear,

are those of Christmas, Hogmanay, New-year's Day, and Handsel Monday. Such of the boys as can pretend to anything like a voice, have for weeks before been thumbing the collection of excellent new songs, which lies like a bunch of rags in the window sole; and being now able to screech up *Barbara Allan*, or T*he wee Cot-house and the wee Kail-yardie*, they determine upon enacting the part of guizards. For this purpose they don old shirts belonging to their fathers, and mount casques of brown paper, shaped so like a mitre, that I am tempted to believe them borrowed from the Abbot of Unreason: attached to this is a sheet of the same paper, which, falling down in front, covers and conceals the whole face, except where holes are made to let through the point of the nose, and afford sight to the eyes and breath to the mouth. Each vocal guizard is, like a knight of old, attended by a kind of humble squire, who assumes the habiliments of a girl, with an old woman's cap and a broomstick, and is styled 'Bessie.' Bessie is equal in no respect, except that she shares fairly in the proceeds of the enterprise. She goes before her principal; opens all the doors at which he pleases to exert his singing powers; and busies herself, during the time of the song, in sweeping the floor with her broomstick, or in playing any other antics that she thinks may amuse the indwellers. The common reward of this entertainment is a halfpenny; but many churlish persons fall upon the unfortunate guizards, and beat them out of the house. Let such persons, however, keep a good watch upon their cabbage-gardens next Hallowe'en!

The term 'Guisers', with variations in the spelling, was widely used for these visitors – who came mostly at night – in the parts of Scotland where Scots/English was spoken. A historical lineage has been suggested, going back through masked touring players in Mystery plays, Yule Guising in the fifteenth-century Scottish court, the French Fêtes de Fous, to the Roman Saturnalia and even further into the past. The historical connections are weak, but the thrill of appearing in disguise, of not being known in one's own community (however complicit others might be in colluding with the deception), is something which is just as potent now as it would have been 2,000 or 20,000 years ago. John Hutton Browne, in *The Golden Days of Youth: a Fife Village in the Past* (1893), describes the pleasures of being in disguise in a rural community:

The days of the old year were few to run. People were on the outlook for the new one, with its joys and anticipations. They were to bury the old one, with its burdens and cares. The custom of 'Guising' was in full force. Men and women, boys and girls, dressed themselves in strange costumes, and blackened their faces, or otherwise disguised them, and went off to village and farm-houses, sang songs, and danced, to the banter and amusement of the onlookers. It was rare fun. Not to be known, and to have an inspection of the household and its surroundings, was a treat in itself. Then the ability and cleverness of those who detected the

'guisers' were something to boast about. Sometimes a strong youth would seize a damsel, and keep her in his clutches until he was sure of her identity, but he might get into trouble by the walking-sticks of the males under whose protection she was placed.

In Fife, New Year's Eve was also commonly called 'Singin' E'en'. Alexander Laing (1876) describes Guising and the widely known rhymes that went with it, in Newburgh, on the south side of the Firth of Tay:

Hogmanay, or Singin' E'en, is … the festival which is most popular in Newburgh among the young. On this, the last evening of the year, the youth of both sexes, as in other parts of Scotland, go about disguised from house to house in bands, singing songs in every house they visit … Many grave consultations are held by the young beforehand as to the special disguises to be worn on Singin' E'en, and it is looked forward to with impatience, and entered upon with a heartiness, which bespeaks thorough enjoyment. The young Guisers, a generation back, were rewarded with a ferl (*feorth-dael* – Anglo-Saxon, fourth part) of oaten cake, many families specially baking them for the purpose. The dole is now mostly bestowed in money, which is paid to the purser of the band, and is divided equally at the conclusion of the evening's peregrinations. The songs sung are sometimes of a kind that are popular at the time, but old and enduring favourites, and old rude rhymes, which have been handed down orally for many generations, never fail to be also sung on that night. Among these latter, the following is the most common, and holds its place most tenaciously:

Rise up gudewife! an dinna be sweir,
An' deal your gear as lang's you're here;
The day'll come whan ye'll be dead,
An' ye'll hae naither meal nor bread.

Lay by your stocks! lay by your stools!
Ye maunna think that we're fules;
We're bairns come to play,
Gie's oor cakes an' lat's away.

From those whose musical powers are not of a high order, the following rhyme, which sets both music and grammar at defiance, is occasionally heard:

Round the midden I whuppit a geese;
I'll sing nae mair till I get a bit piece.

The demands laid out in these rhymes were widely made by Lowland Guisers. They could be seen as simply 'gallus', or potentially more threatening, and they perhaps reflect the fact that the visitors weren't always welcome, although in most places they would be expected and given good hospitality. A song given by Daniel Gorrie (1869) as sung by New Year's Eve night visitors in Orkney (and which closely resembles the thiggers' song from the North-east) is much more generous in spirit. Gorrie talks of the custom 'for companies of men to go from house to house' as something which happened in the past and quotes the first few verses:

Peace be to this buirdly biggin'! [grand house]
We're a' Queen Mary's men,
From the stethe [foundation] unto the riggin',
And that's before our Lady.

This is gude New Year's even nicht —
We're a' Queen Mary's men;
An' we've come here to claim our richt,
And that's before our Lady.

After asking for cheese, drink and butter, the men go on to wish fertility for the animals; then the song concludes:

Here we hae brocht our carrying-horse —
We're a' Queen Mary's men;
A mony a curse licht on his corse;
He'll eat mair meat than we can get;
He'll drink mair drink than we can swink,
And that's before our Lady.

At the conclusion of the song the minstrels were entertained with cakes and ale, and sometimes a smoked goose was set before the company. The singing-men at starting were few in number, but every house visited sent forth fresh relays, and the chorus waxed in volume as the number of voices increased ... The 'carrying-horse,' mentioned in the final verse, was the clown or jester of the party, who suffered himself to be beaten with knotted handkerchiefs, and received double rations as the reward of his folly.

Gorrie's description of the beating of the 'carrying-horse', who he also calls the 'Baldie' has an echo in another custom which we'll meet at the end of this chapter.

A Shetland version of the song, given as a 'New'r Even's Song', was published in 1869 as 'remembered by an old dame'. It keeps the ballad-like refrain of the Orkney song, but before the requests for food begin it speaks, like a Border ballad, of King Henry who's 'a-hunting gane' with his 'merry young men', and then goes on to describe how 'our lady' was dressed with a gold crown, a silver belt, and gold rings 'upon her fingers ten'.

Robert Chambers (1841) gives an account of the same custom in Deerness, Orkney Mainland, at the beginning of the nineteenth century:

In the primitive parish of Deerness, in Orkney, it was customary, at the beginning of the present century, for old and young of the common class of people to assemble in a great band upon the evening of the last day of the year, and proceed upon a round of visits throughout the district. At every house they knocked at the door, and on being admitted, commenced singing, to a tune of its own, a song appropriate to the occasion ...

Chambers goes on to recount the song, which is very like the one in Gorrie's account, and then describes what happens when the song has ended:

The inner door being opened, a tremendous rush took place towards the interior. The inmates furnished a long table with all sorts of homely fare, and a hearty feast took place, followed by copious libations of ale, charged with all sorts of good wishes. The party would then proceed to the next house, where a similar scene would be enacted. Heaven knows how they contrived to take so many suppers in one evening! No slight could be more keenly felt by a Deerness farmer than to have his house passed over unvisited by the New-year singers.

In other places too, the Guisers might cause offence if they didn't call, implying that this was a stingy household. There may also have been the possibility that a visit from them would bring good luck.

While the Guisers would often simply recite a short rhyme or sing a song before claiming their food or cash, they were sometimes expected to do individual turns, or, in a dramatic performance that was widespread in the Lowlands, perform a play. The play was known as 'Galoshins' (with other spellings like 'Galoshans' and 'Galatians'), and sometimes that was also the Guisers' name for themselves, (together with 'Galatian' occasionally being the name of one of the play's characters). The origin of the word has been widely discussed, with a number of possibilities put forward – from the suggestion that 'galoshan' was the sound made by the Guisers' clogs on the cobbles as they went from house to house (galoshes were originally wooden-soled shoes), to an imaginatively exotic link to the Caledonian chieftain Calgacus, who was defeated by the Romans at the battle of Mons Graupius in AD 85.

Robert Chambers (1841) says that the play was performed by boys at Christmas, Hogmanay, New Year's Day and Handsel Monday, to which we could add Hallowe'en.

The performers, who are never less than three, but sometimes as many as six, having dressed themselves, proceed in a band from house to house, generally contenting themselves with the kitchen for an arena, whither, in mansions presided over by the spirit of good-humour, the whole family will resort to witness the spectacle.

Unlike the Guisers who went singing from door to door, and whose costumes were wide-rangingly exotic, the Galoshins dressed according to character. Chambers describes the costumes as he may have known them when he was a boy, in the early nineteenth century, and goes on to give a text of the play, which is probably an amalgam of several versions:

Galatian is (at the royal burgh of Peebles) dressed in a good whole shirt, tied round the middle with a handkerchief, from which hangs a wooden sword. He has a large cocked-hat of white paper, either cut out with little human profiles, or pasted over with penny valentines. The Black Knight is more terrific in appearance, his dress being, if possible, of tartan, and his head surmounted by an old cavalry cap, while his white stockings are all tied round with red tape. A pair of flaming whiskers adds to the ferocity of his aspect. The Doctor is attired in any faded black clothes which can be had, with a hat probably stolen from a neighbouring scarecrow.

Enter TALKING MAN, and speaks:
Haud away rocks, and haud away reels,
Haud away stocks and spinning-wheels.
Redd room for Gorland, and gie us room to sing,
And I will shew you the prettiest thing
That ever was seen in Christmas time.
Muckle head and little wit, stand ahint the door;
But sic a set as we are, ne'er were here before.
– Shew yourself, Black Knight!

Enter BLACK KNIGHT, and speaks:
Here comes in Black Knight, the great king of Macedon,
Who has conquered all the world but Scotland alone.
When I came to Scotland my heart it grew cold,
To see a little nation so stout and so bold –
So stout and so bold, so frank and so free:
Call upon Galatian to fight wi' me.

Enter GALATIAN, and speaks:
Here come I, Galatian; Galatian is my name;
Sword and pistol by my side, I hope to win the game.

BLACK KNIGHT:
The game, sir, the game, sir, it is not in your power;
I'll cut you down in inches in less than half an hour
My head is made of iron, my heart is made of steel,
And my sword is a Ferrara, that can do its duty weel.

(They fight, and Galatian is worsted, and falls.)

Down, Jack, down to the ground you must go.
Oh! oh! what is this I've done?
I've killed my brother Jack, my father's only son.

TALKING MAN:
Here's two bloody champions that never
fought before;
And we are come to rescue him,
and what can we do more?
Now Galatian he is dead, and on
the floor is laid,
And ye shall suffer for it, I'm very
sore afraid.

BLACK KNIGHT:
I'm sure it was not I, sir;
I'm innocent of the crime:
'Twas this young man
behind me, who drew
the sword sae fine.

The YOUNG MAN
answers:
O you awful villain! to
lay the blame on me;
When my two eyes
were shut, sir, when
this young man did
die.

BLACK KNIGHT:
How could your two eyes be shut, when you were looking
on?
How could your two eyes be shut, when their swords
were drawn?
– Is there ever a doctor to be found?

TALKING MAN:
Call in Dr Brown,
The best in all the town.

Enter DOCTOR, and says:
Here comes in as good a doctor as ever Scotland bred,
And I have been through nations, a-learning of my trade;
And now I've come to Scotland all for to cure the dead.

BLACK KNIGHT:
What can you cure?

DOCTOR:
I can cure the rurvy scurvy,
And the rumble-gumption of a man that has been seven years
in his grave or more;
I can make an old woman of sixty look like a girl of sixteen.

BLACK KNIGHT:
What will you take to cure this dead man?

DOCTOR:
Ten pounds.

BLACK KNIGHT:
Will not one do?

DOCTOR:
No.

BLACK KNIGHT:
Will not three do?

DOCTOR:
No.

BLACK KNIGHT:
Will not five do?

DOCTOR:
No.

BLACK KNIGHT:
Will not seven do?

DOCTOR:
No.

BLACK KNIGHT:
Will not nine do?

DOCTOR:
Yes, perhaps – nine may do, and a pint of wine.
I have a little bottle of inker-pinker in my pocket.

Aside to GALATIAN:
Take a little drop of it.
By the hocus-pocus, and the magical touch of my little finger,
Start up, John!

GALATIAN rises, and exclaims:
Oh, my back!

DOCTOR:
What ails your back?

GALATIAN:
There's a hole in't you may turn your nieve [fist] ten times
round in it.

DOCTOR:
How did you get it?

GALATIAN:
Fighting for our land.

DOCTOR:
How many did you kill?

GALATIAN:
I killed a' the loons but ane, that ran, and wadna stand.

The whole party dance, and Galatian sings:
Oh, once I was dead, sir, but now I am alive,
And blessed be the doctor that made me revive.
We'll all join hands, and never fight more,
We'll a' be good brothers, as we have been before.

Enter JUDAS with the bag, and speaks:
Here comes in Judas; Judas is my name;
If ye put not siller in my bag, for guidsake mind our wame!
When I gaed to the castle yett, and tirled at the pin,
They keepit the keys o' the castle, and wadna let me in.
I've been i' the east carse,
I've been i' the west carse,
I've been i' the Carse o' Gowrie,
Where the cluds rain a' day pease and beans,
And the farmers theek houses wi' needles and prins.
I've seen geese gaun on pattens,
And swine fleeing i' the air like peelings o' ingons!
Our hearts are made o' steel, but our bodies sma' as ware
If you've onything to gie us, stap it in there.

FINALE SUNG BY THE PARTY.
Blessed be the master o' this house, and the mistress also,
And all the little babies that round the table grow;
Their pockets full of money, the bottles full of beer –
A merry Christmas, guizards, and a happy New-year.

Versions of this play are found not only in the Scottish Lowlands, but throughout northern, central and southern England, and in Northern Ireland. Folklorists call it a Hero Combat play, and its theme of death and revival once led to a widespread belief that it had its roots in pagan ceremonies, perhaps even in annual human sacrifices that would ensure renewed fertility to the wasteland of winter. But there's no evidence for thinking that the play goes back beyond the early 1700s. It appears to have had its heyday in the nineteenth century, its popularity encouraged because it was printed in chapbooks, cheap pamphlets that were sold at fairs, on street corners, and more recently – up until the 1950s in the north of England (where it was performed widely at Easter) – in town

corner shops. The play's text varies a lot between places, but it generally holds to a basic structure. A clearing of the performance space ('Haud away rocks, haud away reels ...') precedes the introduction of the two (sometimes more) champions. The bad guy, in this case the Black Knight, brags of his prowess like any villain in a Hollywood movie, then goes on to slay the Hero. But help is at hand; a Doctor is called for and, in spite his apparent quackery, he resurrects the Hero, often with nothing more than the touch of a finger and a drop of mysterious liquid from a bottle.

The Galoshins play survived into the twentieth century, in earlier times performed more by young men, but latterly increasingly by boys (girls sometimes took part too). Though its decline was rapid, there were still people living in the 1970s who could remember taking part in it. The text has sometimes been dismissed as doggerel, but in performance, as a piece of popular entertainment, it can be tremendously effective: it has plenty of action; the speeches range from the declamatory heroic to virtuoso comic runs and dialogue, and so can accommodate a range of acting abilities; it works 'in the round', so is perfect for performance in the room of a house, where an audience of all ages and sizes can gather round and see the action; and it serves its primary purpose, which is to entertain well enough to elicit donations of cash from the households in which it is performed.

The last band of strange visitors hails from the west of the Gàidhealtachd. When Samuel Johnson and James Boswell visited Coll in 1773, they were told by the young laird of what Ronald Black describes as 'an aristocratic inversion of the well-known custom of expelling the old year ...' In Boswell's account, 'on the last night of the old year, a man puts upon him a cow's skin and runs round the house, while a number of people make a noise chasing him and beating upon the skin, which sounds like a drum.'

The racket was used to trick visitors into going out into the cold night, egged on by the family, who colluded in the deception. Once outside, no one was allowed back in the house 'without repeating a verse of their own composition'. Those in the know might have been preparing all year for their 'turn'. Robert Chambers got wind of this custom. His description of it, in *The Olio* of 1832, though second hand, is closer than Boswell's to accounts which were gathered later, in the twentieth century. Chambers speaks of:

> A very curious New-Year's-Day custom in the Highlands of Scotland. In many parts of this wild territory, young and old collect on the first night of the year, and perform the following strange ceremony. One of the stoutest of the party drags behind him a dried cow-hide, [he would almost certainly be wearing it on his back] while the rest follow, and beat it with sticks ...

Chambers then gives their song in phonetic Gaelic, followed by a broad English translation:

> Hug man a'
> Yellow bag
> Beat the skin,
> Carlin in neuk,
> Carlin in kirk,
> Carlin ben at the fire,
> Spit in her two eyes,
> Spit in her stomach,
> Hug men a'

After going round the house three times, they all halt at the door, and each person utters an extempore rhyme, extolling the hospitality of the landlord and landlady; after which they are plentifully regaled with bread, butter, cheese, and whisky. Before leaving the house, one of the party burns the breast part of the skin of a sheep, and puts it to the nose of everyone, that all may smell it, as a charm against witchcraft and every infection.

Discussing a similar rhyme given in John Gregorson Campbell's *Witchcraft and Second Sight in the Highlands and Islands* (1902), Ronald Black identifies Chambers' carlin with the *cailleach* (Gaelic for 'old woman') – the last sheaf from the previous harvest which has been kept in the house, waiting for symbolic ritual slaughter at the end of the year; hence the cruel treatment of impaling (the 'spit' being a sharpened stake rather than saliva), reminiscent of the treatment handed out to John Barleycorn in the well-known folk song of the same name.

Alexander Carmichael gives more details of the custom as it was practised during the later nineteenth century, when it seems to have been widespread in the West Highlands and Islands. He explains how the walls of the old houses in the West were between 5 and 8ft thick. The roof was raised from the inner edge of the wall, so the top of the wall could be used as a walkway – and there was access to it through projecting stones by the door, which served as steps:

> When the men come to a house they ascend the wall and run round sunwise, the man in the hide shaking the horns and hoofs, and the other men striking the hard hide with their sticks. The appearance of the man in the hide is gruesome, while the din made is terrific. Having descended and recited their runes at the door, the Hogmanay men are admitted and treated to the best in the house.

This circuit of the wall tops wasn't universal. For example, in other circumstances the *gillean Callaig* – the Hogmanay lads – would enter a house after they had performed their rhyme, and go three times sunwise around the hearth if it was in the middle of the room – as, in earlier times, it generally would have been – or alternatively, around a conveniently placed chair. This is the procedure described by Donald MacDonald in an interview recorded in 1980, in which he describes the custom in North Tolsta, in his native Lewis, as it was carried on between Christmas Eve and Hogmanay until after the First World War. There, bands of boys, aged between about seven and fifteen, would go around the villages, one of them with a dried sheepskin or calfskin on his back, secured by a loop around his neck. In a big village there might be a number of bands with an average of fifteen or so boys in each, and they would try not to encroach on each other's territory. After the boys had gained entrance to a house, they would make their circuit three times round the fire, all the time chanting their rhyme, while the dwellers in the house would try to hit the hide 'with sticks, with the tongs even' or just with their hands. The boys collected gifts of food from each household in a couple of sacks and, when they had gathered as much as they could, they would go to the house of one of the spinsters who lived in the village, who would help them to divide up their spoils. Any surplus, they would give to her.

Robert Chambers suggests that the burning of the strip of sheep's breast meat was used to produce purifying smoke. Often it did serve this purpose, put under the noses of everyone in the household – but occasionally it was eaten, for in some places it was reckoned to be the tastiest part of the beast.

Here is a vibrant account of the custom, translated by his son from the Gaelic prose writings of Reverend Norman MacLeod (1783 – 1862), who put the words in the mouth of the piper to the Camerons of Glendessary:

> The time of *Calluinn* came, when someone had to carry the dry cow hide on his back and run round the house, and every one

that could, tried to get a stroke at it with his stick. 'Who will carry the hide this year?' says Evan Ban. 'Who but Para Mor?' (Big Patrick) says one. 'Who but Broad John?' says another. 'Out with the hide Para Mor,' says Evan Ban, 'and you Broad John, stand by his shoulder in case he may stumble.' Para Mor drew the hide about his head, taking a twist of the tail firmly around his fist. '*Cothrom na Feinne*' (i.e fair play as among the Fingalians, or Fingalian justice), exclaimed he, as he drew near the door of the house where the Laird (*Fear a' bhaile*, the man of the place) was standing with his Caman (shinty) in his hand. '*Calluinn* here!' says he, giving the first rattle to the hide. Para Mor set off, but, swift of foot as he was, the men of the Glen kept at his heel, and you would think that every flail in the country was at work on the one threshing-floor, as every mother's son of them struck and rattled at him, shouting, '*a Calluinn* here! The *Calluinn* of the yellow sack of hide! Strike ye the skin! A *Calluinn* here!' Three times they went *Deas-iul* (in a southerly direction, according to the course of the sun) around the house.

7

SPORT
AND PLAY

New Year's Day is still an important time for sport in Scotland, but before the First World War the whole country – mainland and islands – echoed with the shouts of spectators and participants, in games and combative contests which could involve whole communities, either as players or onlookers.

Robert Chambers (1869) describes some of the gentler pursuits. Curling was very popular. He sees it as a great social leveller:

> ... in a small community, the curling *rink* is usually surrounded by persons of all classes – the laird, the minister, and the provost, being all hail-fellow-well-met on this occasion with the tailors, shoemakers, and weavers, who at other times never meet them without a reverent vailing of the beaver. Very often a plain dinner of boiled beef with *greens* concludes the merry-meeting.

Chambers, sketching a scene that would delight a *Punch* cartoonist, says that skating was also a favourite amusement, '...nor do the boys fail to improve the time by forming slides on lake, on pond, yea, even on the public highways, notwithstanding the frowns of old gentlemen and the threatenings of policemen.'

In many New Year sports, rivalry between communities was a prominent feature. Allan Cunningham (1834) tells of conflict between the lads of Ecclefechan and those of Lockerbie:

> Ecclefechan is a little thriving village in Allandale: nor is it more known for its hiring fairs than for beautiful lasses and active young men. The latter, when cudgel-playing was regularly taught to the youth of the Scottish lowlands, distinguished themselves by skill and courage; they did not,

however, enjoy their fame without contention: they had frequent feuds with the lads of Lockerby, and their laurels were put in jeopardy. On an Old New Year's-day, some thirty years ago, Ecclefechan sent some two hundred 'sticks' against Lockerby: they drew themselves up beside an old fortalice and intimated their intention of keeping their post until the sun went down: they bit their thumbs, flourished their oak saplings, and said, 'We wad like to see wha wad hinder us.' This was a matter of joy to the lads of Lockerby: an engagement immediately took place, and Ecclefechan seemed likely to triumph, when – I grieve to write it – a douce elder of the kirk seizing a stick from one who seemed unskilful in using it – rushed forward, broke the enemy's ranks, pushed the lads of Ecclefechan rudely out of the place, and exclaimed, 'That's the way we did lang syne!'

A vast range of sports and games crops up in newspaper reports or memoirs about New Year during the nineteenth and early twentieth centuries: shooting and ploughing matches, gambling with cards – sometimes for nights on end – boules, quoits, angling, tug-of-war, carpet bowling, golf, athletics. The New Year Sprint, formerly known as 'the Powderhall' after the Edinburgh stadium where it began, has been run since 1870, the era of hugely popular pedestrian galas, or foot-racing competitions. A handicap race over 110m, it remains a prestigious sporting event. There were model boat races and regattas, for instance on Shetland, Mull and on the island of Stroma in the Pentland Firth. In Caithness a game called 'Knotty' (another name for shinty) was played by knocking a ball around with cabbages swung by their stalks.

Outdoor swims, usually for charity and often in fancy dress, are today a popular New Year's Day activity. In Scotland the best known is The Loony Dook, now part of the official Edinburgh Hogmanay programme. It began on a small scale in 1987, and now over 1,000 participants parade through the small town of South Queensferry before plunging into the River Forth against the photogenic backdrop of the Forth Railway Bridge.

Further north, on the Tay Estuary, is the longest-running mass splash to welcome the New Year. Ye Amphibious Ancients Bathing Association was formed in Broughty Ferry in 1889 to encourage open water bathing, and its minute book of 1891 records a Ne'er Day swim by a handful of local people. 'The Phibbies', as they are known, have kept this as part of their year-round programme ever since, and are now joined annually by hundreds of enthusiasts.

These dookers – plus many others in smaller events around the country – take to the water during daylight. So, contenders for the hardiest were surely four members of the Aberdeen Sea Swimming Club, pictured in 1948 by the local paper towelling themselves dry in the early hours of 1 January, after 'first-footing' the North Sea as the clock struck twelve.

For Highlanders, whether on their native heath or departed for the city, the most celebrated of the New Year sports was shinty. *The Celtic Monthly*, 1896:

> Many romantic stories are associated with the observance of the time honoured shinty match on New Year's Day in the north. In the south, the Highlanders keep up the custom and in Glasgow, Edinburgh and London the local shinty clubs never fail to engage in a game of caman, followed perhaps by a dance on the green to celebrate the birth of another year.

Shinty is closely related to the Irish sport of hurling, and it's been suggested that it was brought over from Ireland by Christian missionaries and early settlers. Shinty was once played over the whole of Scotland and is now well-regulated, with an internationally agreed set of rules. But until the end of the nineteenth century, with the formation of the Camanachd Society, it was played in different areas according to local rules. In earlier times the essence of the game – played by opposing sides of able-bodied men, each of whom was equipped with a wooden club (*caman* in Gaelic) – was to propel a ball which was generally made from a single knot of wood to the goal, or *hail*, at one end or the other of a pitch that could sometimes extend over a wide area. A favoured location for a game of shinty was the beach, and a game could last for the best part of a day, or until the tide came in.

Martin Martin, who visited St Kilda in 1697, describes how shinty was played there:

> They use for their diversion short clubs and balls of wood; the sand is a fair field for this sport and exercise, in which they take great pleasure, and are very nimble at it; they play for eggs, fowl, hooks, or tobacco; and so eager are they for victory that they strip themselves to their shirts to obtain it …

Declaring that 'this is undoubtedly the game of the Gael,' Robert Craig Maclagan, who devotes almost fifteen pages to the sport in *The Games & Diversions of Argyleshire* (1901), says that, while shinty was played often during December and January, 'on New Year's Day great crowds turned out to the various shinty fields, all ages, boys, young men, and men even of sixty and upwards'. He goes on:

> There were places well known as shinty grounds in the various localities. In Islay the 'Machair' of Balinaby was one of the most famous. It is still in the recollection of some when there were here gathered on New Year's morning crowds of players, cheered by the presence of six or seven pipers, play being carried on during the whole day, with the late Lairds of Islay and of Balinaby superintending, of course, both in the kilt, as was the fashion with Campbell of Islay [the renowned folklorist]. One reciter has lively recollections of two men,

MacNiven and MacLauchlan, both old and grey-haired at the time, but recognised as distinguished players, taking a prominent part. They divested themselves of nearly every article of clothing; their feet were bare, with a handkerchief tied round their heads, yet wet with perspiration.

On these occasions others not playing amused themselves in groups dancing to the pipes.

In the early 1930s, Reverend Coll A. MacDonald wrote a letter to his son who had emigrated to America, describing the last New Year shinty match on the island of Iona.

Alain, a'ghraidh (Dear Alan)

When you were a little fellow of twelve you accompanied me to Iona and I was anxious that you should fall under its spell. But I was not satisfied that the island captured your heart. You wanted to know how people could pass their years there. I did not tell you then but now that you have reached manhood, I will tell you.

To you, 1881 is remote but I was there in my eighth year and while I remember many things that happened before that day, such as the great storm that destroyed the Tay Bridge, 1881 stands out as the year of the last shinty match on New Year's Day. I have seen many interesting contests, and you have seen the excited crowds at international matches, but all these later events pale before the shinty match of 1st January 1881.

Your grandfather, known as Big Donald, captained one side and Richard Sinclair led the others. The physical contrast between the two men appeared ridiculous. It was as if one of the giants at Oban Games had, in the hammer-throwing contest, Harry Lauder as his opponent. Your grandfather was a burly weight, no taller than you but massive as a Viking. He was too heavy for speed or agility but in strength and power of endurance he was a Hercules. He was then forty-three years of age and weighed eighteen stones. If you have seen A.A.Cameron, the Lochaber giant, you can form a fair idea of what your grandfather would have been if he had gymnasium training. Richard Sinclair was a small dark man, about fifty years of age and weighing about nine stones. But Sinclair was wiry and active and made up in shrewdness and skill what he lacked in height and weight.

Though the match was played one afternoon, it was not a one-day affair as you may think. For weeks the youth and manhood played shinty, talked shinty, dreamed shinty. In Iona the winter is never cold. The wind may blow with all the fury of Atlantic gales, but the air is balmy and the ground but rarely frost-bound. There were camans to secure and there was no Lumley or Ivor Anderson to provide them. They came from the hazel woods of the Ross of Mull. If it takes the eye of a sculptor to see in the block of marble a Venus or Apollo, it takes an expert woodsman to see the well-shaped caman in the uncouth block of wood. The skilled makers of clubs were real craftsmen, with all the joy of creative art as they shaped the weapons of the young generation.

At last the morning dawned. The sky was grey and a gentle breeze blew from the west, a soft balmy wind such as blows only in the Hebrides in January. At noon the whole male population flocked to the scene of play above Ceann na Creige. What a scene for the Homeric combat! The Atlantic breakers, with unhurried rhythmical swish, beat upon the shore where the gravelly beach made a strange musical sound as the pebbles rolled seaward with each receding wave. On the landward side lay Lochan Mhic an Aoig. Between these east and west boundaries stretched the sandy Machair, soft and kindly to the tread as any carpet that ever graced a Persian palace. The southerly goal-posts lay as near the rising ground as possible and the northern goal-posts lay in the hollow beneath the brow of Cnoc na Maoile Buidhe, the hill of the yellow brow.

The teams were only limited by the number of adults and youths of playing capacity. The risk of disturbing the peace by a game on New Year's Day was not to be left out of the reckoning. No-one lost caste, however much whisky he consumed on that day. I would not have you infer they were a drunken generation. But on the opening day of the year there was a special licence and men frequently indulged who were very abstemious for the rest of the year.

But on 1st January 1881 it was a sober crowd that covered the velvety sward above Ceann na Creige. They denied themselves like Grecian athletes who strove for mastery at the Olympic Games. Whatever may have been the evening potations, the men were temperate in all things in the morning. The captains tossed a coin and fortune favoured your grandfather. He, thinking more of kinship than of speed or brawn, eagerly claimed his kinsman, Neil MacDonald. I do not mean that Neil lacked skill as an exponent of the game of shinty, but I am certain that was not the deciding factor in your grandfather's choice. Richard Sinclair, with characteristic shrewdness, selected Neil MacArthur, a powerful young seaman who was certain to give of his best against our clan. Your grandfather's second choice was John MacAulay who was expected to exert himself to defeat his employer. And then, with a roguish twinkle in his eye, Richard Sinclair hailed your uncle John to his side. He was fleet of foot, accurate of eye and tireless in energy. He proved a sound investment for Richard Sinclair.

Men of fifty and youths of twelve stood around their respective captains. Then came the choice of ends and in a day of gentle breezes it made little difference which won. A shinty was tossed in the air and the age-long shout of *cas no bas* (head or handle) decided the direction of play. There was neither sawdust line nor chalk mark to disfigure the green plain. The sea was the boundary on one side and the little loch on the other. The players streamed out like the caddies at St Andrews when the captain of the year plays himself into office. The leaders stood in mid-field and he who won the toss of the coin was asked whether the ball – a wooden one – was to be thrown on the ground or cast in the air. The old formula was *athar no talamh* (air or earth). If the ball is cast in the air the taller man is likely to get the first blow, while greater equality reigns if the ball is cast on the ground. I do not think there was any referee, the ball was in play and the great game began.

What racing and chasing of that small ball! There were too many players engaged to make scoring easy. My recollection is that there were neither backs nor halves. All were forward and first but, as the too eager combatants tired and rested to recover breath, there were cute ones who hung on the wings and made fast runs that thrilled the onlookers. Though more than the half-century has passed, I can still see two bearded warriors on the sea side of the plain whose speed filled my boyish eyes with wonder and delight. They were Calum Cameron and his cousin John Campbell. Both were in their stocking soles and their fast runs made a magnificent spectacle. It mattered not which was in control of the ball, the other overtook and dispossessed him. Like Achilles and Hector on the plains of Troy, the great Atlantic their Scamander, first the one and then the other prevailed. If they had only centred the ball as it was carried towards the goal, many hails would have counted. But each stuck grimly to the ball till he was dispossessed by numbers. When your grandfather's goal was threatened, he fell back to protect it and, though he could be rounded, he could not be cast aside. Time and again his vast bulk and Herculean might stemmed the tide.

At length, when it seemed as if no hail was to come, his own son John swerved past his father and scored a clean, clear hail. The Machair rang with the joyous shout. Shintys were tossed in the air in ecstasy of joy. The combat was renewed. The losers redoubled their efforts and the winners set themselves with grim determination to hold their lead. No one was tired now. Faster and faster grew the play. Shintys were smashed into splinters and, with the stumps only, that elusive ball travelled from end to end. They seemed to have no time limit any more than a limit in space. It looked as if only the darkness of the short winter day would end the fight.

But big John MacAulay now got possession for your grandfather's side and from mid-field drove a ball with such speed and power that no weapon could stay its flight. Like an arrow it sped between the posts and Sinclair's fortress fell. The great game was ended: it was a draw.

MacAulay was the guest of honour at your grandfather's table that evening. The bottle that was in little demand in the morning journeyed from end to end of the table many times. Tales of great games on Traigh Sanna and Saorphin were heard and we, of immature age, listened spellbound while our seniors related the history of the heroes of their youth, now on Canadian plains or 'neath the Southern Cross. Song and story chased each other to the end of a perfect day.

The act of transporting a ball – or some similar object – to one end or the other of a large pitch as a contest between two communities, or two opposing parts of the same community, is ancient and widespread. Before the middle of the nineteenth century, when rugby and football started to become standardised into their current forms, mass ball games were quite common, played at particular times of the year, in England, Scotland and France. In England, Shrove Tuesday was a popular day for these games, though they also took place at weddings, at Christmas and Easter, and on the days of dedication of parish saints. There could be up to 2,000 people taking part, divided into two or more teams, which might consist of members of different parishes, the opposing supporters of specific leaders, or the married men versus the bachelors of a parish. It was mainly a man's sport, though, in at least one place in Scotland, married women competed against spinsters.

Mass football began to die out with the nineteenth century, to some degree at least, because its violence was proscribed. In Derby, for example, in 1846, the street football contest had developed into a battle between the parishes of All Saints' and St Peter's, and it took two troops of dragoons, a large band of special constables, and a reading of the Riot Act to quell the violence. A handful of games in this old style are still played in Britain, and the best known in Scotland is the Kirkwall Ba' game, played between the Uppies and the Doonies in the streets of the Orkney capital. In *Summers and Winters in the Orkneys* (1869), Daniel Gorrie describes the game as he witnessed it in Victorian Kirkwall:

The game – which should have ended with the era of cockfighting – is virtually a trial of strength, of pushing and wrestling power between 'up the street' and 'down the street,' the grand object of the belligerents being to propel the ball to one or the other end of the town. Broad Street, where the struggle commences under the shadow of St. Magnus [Cathedral], becomes the centre of attraction about noon-tide. Sailors and porters arrive in formidable force from the purlieus of the harbour, tradesmen gather in groups, and even hoary-headed men, feeling the old glow of combative blood in their veins, hasten to the scene

of anticipated contest. At one o'clock a signal pistol-shot is fired, the ball is tossed into the air from the steps of the old cross, and around it, soon as it bumps on the ground, there immediately gathers from all sides a dense and surging crowd. The wrestling and struggling mass sways hither and thither, sometimes revolving like a maelstrom, and at other times stationary in a grim dead-lock.

At intervals, the ball, as if flying for dear life, makes a spasmodic bound from the crowd; but a sudden headlong rush encloses it again, and so the struggle continues as before. For onlookers it is exciting to observe the fierce red-hot faces of the combatants, while the only appearance of good-humour displayed is a grim smile flickering fitfully across an upturned visage. It is curious also to note the eager, uneasy motions, outside the revolving ring, of men long past their prime, who were wont to be in the centre of the crowd in other years. Heavy knock-down blows, both foul and fair, are freely given and received. The struggle seldom lasts much longer than an hour, and when the seamen and porters win the day, they place the ball, as a trophy of conquest, on the top-mast of the largest ship in the harbour.

Nearly a century and a half later, the Kirkwall Ba' game has essentially remained unchanged. It's now played on both Christmas Day and New Year's Day. Tom Muir, storyteller and Orcadian native, was once bold enough to take part in the game himself:

The Ba' in Kirkwall has been raging through the streets for over 200 years, but before that it was played since medieval times just on the outskirts of the town (now Dundas Crescent). I am an Uppie by birth, but both my parents were Doonies. Coming from the North Isles they first landed in the town at the pier where the Doonie's goal is situated. But as a country boy I didn't join in, as many Kirkwallians actually object to our presence; it's a Kirkwall game. I did, however, have a go on New Year's Day 1982, and never again! You find yourself sucked helplessly into the scrum of players and then being lifted off the ground as the players behind shove their shoulders into the scrum and push upwards. You dangle there, the life being squeezed out of you, and you can't move. There is no point saying 'Excuse me, would you mind letting me out, please?' That will cut no mustard with the real Ba' players.

I have heard people say that the Ba' game is a drunken orgy, but nothing could be further from the truth. If a drunk tried to join in the Ba' they would be unceremoniously ejected and told to keep their distance. To the serious Ba' player a drunk is a nuisance and a menace to themselves. The last thing that you want to do in the scrum is fall over; that could have serious consequences. The dedicated Ba' player has sworn to forego the delights of Christmas and Hogmanay to focus his full attentions on the game. Christmas dinner with the family is eaten on Boxing Day, while all Hogmanay drinking is left until after the game is over when you either celebrate or drown your sorrows, depending on the result. The idea of going into the Ba' with a hangover is an ordeal that no one would relish.

The crowd gathers on the street for the throw up of the men's Ba' at one o'clock. The person given the honour of throwing up the Ba' from the Market Cross in front of St Magnus Cathedral chats to friends; quite often they are former Ba' winners themselves and they reminisce about the time that they won the coveted Ba'. Then, like medieval armies taking the field of battle, the two teams, the Uppies and the Doonies, come striding from the territory that marks their own half of the town. There are some good natured handshakes before the battle commences. Time seems to pass slowly as you wait for the bell of St Magnus Cathedral to strike the hour. As soon as it is heard, the Ba' is thrown up and sails through the air in an arc towards the sea of outstretched hands that are waiting to get that first touch of it. It soon disappears into the scrum and is lost from view. It might not make an appearance again until the end, when it either hits the Uppies wall or is thrown into the cold water of Kirkwall Basin.

Once the scrum has been on the street for some time you see a column of steam rising from it in the cold air, as the temperature inside rises. Spectators carry bottles of water and pass them to the men inside, if they get the chance of moving nearer the edge of the scrum. One visiting spectator once remarked on seeing the steam rising from the scrum, 'Oh, look! Are they having a barbeque?' Inside the scrum the pressure is unrelenting. One year the Ba' went down a small lane called Gunn's Close, which has houses on one side and a 5ft high drystone wall on the other with a car park behind it. The pressure of the scrum was so intense that it burst through the wall. One stalwart of the Ba' once suffered cracked ribs, which is not uncommon. He went to the hospital where the doctor eyed him with suspicion and not much sympathy. On reading the patient's notes he exclaimed, 'Good god! You were in here exactly a year ago with the same injuries.' It was then explained to him that he had been playing in a traditional game and the doctor declared that he must go and see it for himself after his shift finished.

A friend of mine once told me that you would punch your best friend in the mouth if he had the Ba' and was on the opposite team, but once it was all over you returned to being friends and all animosity was forgotten. This was not always the case with the spectators though. My father had a cousin, also a Doonie, called Mary. She had three great passions in her life: booze, poodles and the Ba'. She was often to be seen on the outside of the scrum shouting encouragement (and abuse) at the players, but she liked to be a bit more 'hands on' in her support. She would whack the Uppie players over the back with her walking stick and it was said that she even used to stab them in the calves with hat pins!

The men's game can last for many hours, leaving the players exhausted at the end of play. Once it has reached the winning goal, a discussion (sometimes heated) is held to decide who should win the Ba'. The winner is given the Ba' to take home with them and keep; a new Ba' is made for every game. Another friend of mine who won a Ba' was so happy that he took it to bed with him that night.

Back in the 1960s the local newspaper, *The Orcadian*, was predicting the end of the Ba' as player numbers dwindled. This has proved an unfounded fear as the number of men playing is now as high as it has ever been. The Millennium Ba' was a cause for concern, as it was worried that there would be a boost in numbers from people who were not regular Ba' players but just people wanting to say that they had played in it. It was a very big Ba', with a huge crowd of spectators and TV film crews from all over the world, but it all went off without a problem. But the Ba' has a secret weapon; The Ba' Committee. These dedicated individuals go into the schools to talk to the boys who will be playing in the Boys' Ba', which takes place in the morning at 10 a.m. They drive home the fact that players need to be responsible and to help any player who falls or is injured, as well as to respect people and property. Respect is held up as an important factor in the Ba'

game and teaches good manners to the boys who will be the future men's Ba' players.

The Ba' has gone from strength to strength over the years and is still held with great affection in the hearts of not just Kirkwall residents, but the people of Orkney. It has had its moments of controversy, like recently when it was swept away into a car which raced up to the Uppies goal. Since the game has no rules as such, this was allowed, but even many Uppies condemned it as unsporting. No such recurrence happened during this season's games, I am happy to report. It is a great piece of Orkney's heritage and tradition, and long may it be played through the streets of the old town.

Though, after a decline, shinty has held its own, and is currently growing in popularity, the inexorable rise of football from the end of the nineteenth century, to become the national game, has seen an end to mass ball games in all but a handful of places (as well as Kirkwall, there's a Candlemas game at Jedburgh, and a summer game in the market place in Duns in Berwickshire). Violence on and off the field is not uncommon today, but here is a report, headlined 'A Soldiers' Riot', from the *Aberdeen Daily Journal* on 4 January 1912, of a situation where New Year conviviality seems to have become entangled with national pride and the spirit of the more riotous of the old Ba' games to produce a volatile situation which quickly became the stuff of legend:

The accounts of the disturbances which occurred at the instructional camp for mounted infantry at Longmoor in Hampshire differ materially in regard to details, but all agree as to the extraordinary character of the outbreak.

The earliest news was to the effect that the Scottish soldiers, having been refused the opportunity of celebrating the New Year, by way of retaliation sallied forth from their quarters at midnight, armed with belts, bayonets, rifles and stones and after badly wrecking several of their own huts, proceeded to the officers' quarters, where they made a hostile demonstration, chiefly by way of smashing windows. Surprised at the noise, the officers rushed outside, the guard was called out and a furious melee occurred, the occasional snap of a rifle being heard above the din. The result was that one man was shot in the head, other men were wounded and more windows were broken. Finally, a resourceful officer resorted to the expedient of challenging a man to single combat, and in the rather Gilbertian fashion of a battle of fisticuffs the ugly episode came to an end.

Fortunately, it would appear that this report is very much overcoloured. That the Scotsmen harboured no ill-feeling over the matter of the New Year festivities is evident from the fact that at midnight on Sunday they marched to the Commandant's quarters and serenaded him, singing 'Auld Lang Syne' and 'Jolly Good Fellow' and giving him three rousing cheers. The truth would seem to be that the whole unpleasant incident arose out of feeling engendered over nothing more serious than the result of a football match in which a Scottish team, pitted against Devon men, were beaten.

The Commandant's account is that on New Year's night a section of a Scottish Company and a section of the Yorkshire Regiment quarreled over the match, that a fight took place which lasted for little more than a quarter of an hour, that two men were wounded, with a knife or possibly a bayonet, and that a number of windows were broken.

If the first report exaggerates the occurrence, this account probably unduly minimises it. But while the disturbance seems undoubtedly to have been serious, and is much to be deplored, it is very satisfactory for the credit of the troops to be able to believe that it can in no sense be described as a mutiny against authority.

8

THE OTHER WORLD

Hallowe'en and Midwinter are the two seasons in the annual calendar when the door to the Other World is most likely to be open; when some aspects of the future can be spied through a crack in the door; and when the beings who dwell on either side of the threshold can cross into each other's realms.

Fortune-telling at Hallowe'en seems to have been preoccupied largely with the question of marriage and who one's future partner would be. Robert Burns devotes a whole poem to the different ways in which this can be determined, though he doesn't mention anything resembling the New Year practice in Islay, reported at the end of the nineteenth century by Robert Maclagan:

> It was a custom with young people … on the night of the New Year to take the bealag (smelt) of a herring and throw it against the ceiling or wall. If it would stick, it was a sign that the person who threw it would be married within the year; but if it fell, there would be no marriage that year. If the bealag lay straight where it struck, the person to whom the thrower was to be married was to be handsome but if it lay bent or twisted, it indicated that the marriage would be to a bent or deformed person.

New Year's Night was also a time to predict how the weather would turn out in the following year. In *The Statistical Account of Scotland* of 1794, the minister of Kirkmichael, in Banffshire, describes how the people of his parish looked to the direction of the wind for guidance:

> The wind from the South will be productive of heat and fertility; the wind of the West of milk and fish; the wind from the North of cold and storm; the wind from the East of fruit on the trees.

In *The Popular Superstitions and Festive Amusements of the Highlanders of Scotland* (1823), W. Grant Stewart records the appearance in the sky at New Year of 'that admirable object of Highland curiosity, the "Candlemas Bull"', whose significance seems to be 'prognostic of its being a good or a bad year':

> He has, it is said, neither wings nor any other apparent buoyants; but he takes advantage of the course of the wind, on which he glides along in fellowship with the clouds, in a manner that would do credit to the best aeronaut of the day.

Grant Stewart confesses that, never having seen the bull himself, he can't say where it rises and sets in the sky, or what it looks like in any detail:

> All our informants, however, agree in representing it as of a very large size, the colour of a dark cloud, and having all the limbs of a common bull.

Reverend Walter Gregor (1881) gives some examples of divination at New Year, including ways of prediction which depended, as in Banffshire, on the direction of the wind:

> The last thing done on the last day of the year was to 'rist' the fire, that is, cover up the live coals with the ashes. The whole was made as smooth and neat as possible. The first thing on New Year's morning was to examine if there was in the ashes any mark like the shape of a human foot with the toes pointing towards the door. If there was such a mark, one was to be removed from the family before the year was run. Some climbed to the roof of the house and looked down the 'lum' for the dreaded mark.
>
> The first fire was carefully watched. If a peat or a live coal rolled away from it, it was regarded as an indication that a member of the family was to depart during the year.
>
> Some there were who laid claim to divine what kind the coming harvest was to be from the appearance of the stars during the last night of the year. From the way in which the wind blew on New Year's Day auguries were drawn whether the crop of beans and peas would be good or bad during that year.

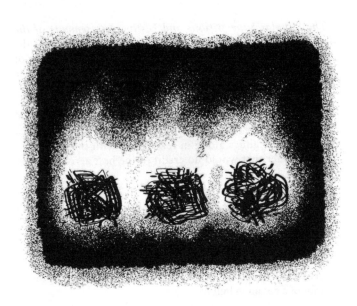

As well as being a time for divination, New Year was a time when Trows were at large, when the doors to fairy knolls opened, and when standing stones could walk. In *Rambles in the Far North* (1884), R. Menzies Fergusson relates two tales from Orkney which might have come from an unpublished story by M.R. James:

In the ... parish of Birsay there is one of these Druidical Stones, with a rather strange and tragic history attached to it. The legend runs that every Hogmanay night, as the clock strikes the hour of twelve, this stone begins to walk or move towards Birsay Loch. When the edge of the loch is reached it quietly dips its head into the rippling waters. Then, to remain firm and immovable until the next twelve months pass away, it as silently returns to its post. It was never considered safe for any one to remain out of doors at midnight, and watch its movements upon Hogmanay. Many stories are current of curious persons who dared to watch the stone's proceedings, and who the next morning were found lying corpses by its side. The latest story of the kind is that of a young gentleman from Glasgow, who formed the resolution to remain up all night, and find out for himself the truth or falsehood about this

wonderful stone. One Hogmanay accompanied only by the cold silvery beams of the moon, the daring youth began his watch. As time wore on and the dread hour of midnight approached, he began to feel some little terror in his heart, and an eerie feeling crept slowly over his limbs. At midnight he discovered that, in his pacing to and fro, he had come between the stone and the loch; and as he looked towards the former he fancied that he saw it move. From that moment he lost all consciousness, and his friends found him in the grey dawn lying in a faint. By degrees he came to himself, but he could not satisfy enquirers whether the stone had really moved and knocked him down on its way, or whether his imagination had conjured up the assault.

There is another tale, of a more tragic nature, related of this walking stone. One stormy December day a vessel was shipwrecked upon the shore of Birsay, and all hands save one were lost. The rescued sailor happened to find refuge in a cottage close by this stone; and, hearing the story of its yearly march, he resolved to see for himself all that human eyes might be able to discover. In spite of all remonstrances, he sallied forth on the last night of the old year; and, to make assurance doubly sure, he seated himself on the very pinnacle of the stone. There he awaited the events of the night. What these were no mortal man can tell; for the first morning of the new year dawned upon the corpse of the gallant sailor lad, and local report has it that the walking stone rolled over him as it proceeded to the loch.

In Shetland, the Trows were abroad for the whole of the Yule period, for more than a month from Tulya's E'en, seven days before Yule-day, until Up-helly-a, the twenty-fourth night after. Jessie Saxby (1931) has two stories which emphasise the care humans must take during this time:

One Yule evening a young couple wished to share the merriment in a neighbour's house. They did not wish to be encumbered with their little ones, so they bribed the boys (wee things of three and four years of age) with extra cake and sweets, and put them early to bed, sure that their sleep would be long and fast. As soon as the little eyes closed the youthful parents stole away to join the dancers in the neighbour's house.

The big barn had, as was usual, been cleared for the dancing, and after a few reels the couple adjourned ben-the-hoose to partake of the refreshments.

Shortly after they left the barn there glided into it two tiny creatures scantily attired, with wide open blue eyes, and smiling lips which never said a word.

A shout arose from the youths and maidens, and the older folk laughed. Then one old man said: 'Come awa' me lambs,

and ye sall hae a reel as well as the best of them.' The fiddler struck up 'The Shoals o' Foula,' and the two wee uninvited guests tripped merrily up and down, their small, bare feet keeping time, and executing such marvellous steps that the onlookers declared they must have been taught by the Trows, who are most fine dancers.

When the reel was at its height the young mother returned to the barn, and no sooner did she catch sight of the tiny couple than she exclaimed: 'Gude save wiz, me bairns.' No Trow can remain visible when a pious word is spoken. No sooner had the 'Gude save wiz' passed her lips, than the little strangers vanished through the crowd of lads near the door. Jokes were tossed at the mother but she declared she had left the boys sound asleep in bed.

Snow was on the ground and more was falling. The mother hastened to follow the children, but when she reached her house they were not there. No! nor were they found in any neighbouring house, and then the old folk whispered about the 'Finis' that appears before death, personating the dying individual.

It was all very startling, very terrible, very sad.

For some time the parents and the whole party of merry-makers searched for the children without success.

Then folk whispered of the wonderful steps the little couple had danced, and the curious silence they had maintained. At last an aged dame asked the distracted mother: 'Did do look weel to the sainin'?'

'I never tocht o' it,' cried the terrified girl. 'I never minded upon what should be done at Yule time to sain the bairns.'

So then all the folk kent it was the Trows that had taken the form of Magnie's boys.

There was no more dancing that night, nor for many Yules after in that toon, for next morning the baby boys were found dead in each other's arms in a great, soft snow-drift which filled a ravine not many hundred yards from their home. There was a deep peat mire at the bottom of the ravine, and the children had sunk through the snow into that.

It was a very plain matter, but all the people affirmed that the calamity came through the parents having omitted to sain the bairns on Yule E'en.

* * * *

One Neuersmas a large party had assembled at the Moolapund, and after the evening was half spent, they found that their drink supply was about done, for double the number of people had come than was expected.

Invitations to those entertainments were not given. It was made known that the boys were going to gather at that house on that particular evening. Each man brought a 'drap in the bottle,' and each girl carried some scones and cakes. The older neighbours sent presents to add to the feast.

'Lads,' said the man of the house, 'some o' you will have to go over the hill for a drap to wet wir mooths. My stock has run oot, and forbye, you must get some sweeties for the lasses.'

'You'll meet the Trows about the Moolaburn,' cried a saucy damsel. 'Is do no' feared to speak o' the Grey folk?' whispered a youth in her ear. 'Not I,' retorted the girl. 'Then come with me over the Moolaburn,' he said, 'and see them linkin' ower the braes.' Then before she could answer, he said to the man of the house: 'Maunce, I'll go for a drink and the sweeties, and bonnie Breta here is going to follow me. It's a fine night for a little walk.'

Of course the lads and lasses laughed, and the gudeman wrapped a warm shawl about the girl, and bade young Josey take heed, and not stay long. But as they left the house, an old woman muttered, 'Gude preserve them. It was a füle thing of Breta to speak so lightly o' them that has leave to be aboot the earth this night.'

Long, long did the folk wait and many were the wrathful words uttered at Josey's delay.

At last he came – and came alone! Nay, more, he reeled in flourishing two empty bottles and shouting madly: 'The Trows have got the drink, and they've ta'en the lass too.' All was confusion at once. Josey would have had the bottles cracked upon his head if the loss of the whiskey had been the worst. But Breta, what had become of her? That was a far more important matter. Vainly did the men strive to elicit information from Josey. He was utterly mad with drink and fear, and could only scream between tears and howls: 'The Trows have ta'en me lass. Oh! The Trows! The Trows!' – 'and', said the nurse who told me the story, 'Josey spoke the word o' truth for a' that. Puir Breta was lying idda Moolaburn when her brothers fand her. She had in her hand a bulwand, and that ye ken is what the grey men use for horses. She was dead, puir lass, and all for speakin' lightly o' them that is given power at certain times. As for Josey, he never did more good frae that nicht, and afore the Yules cam round next year he was awa'.'

The story of The Man Who Kicked the Bone, which Alec Williamson learned from his father, tells of a man who was desperate for company one Hogmanay and, as a result, was paid a call by an unlikely visitor:

A very long time ago in the Highlands, this man came into the community. He arrived at a piece of land and there was a house on it. He was a crofter. He wasn't married, he was on his own and he had a housekeeper. He was quite pleased with the croft; he had cattle and sheep and probably a horse or two. But the people there were a bit distant. The housekeeper said to him, 'There's a funeral here tomorrow and by going to the funeral you'll meet some of the neighbours. Tomorrow, yes that's New Year's Eve - Hogmanay we call it here.'

'Aye,' he said, 'I call it Hogmanay also. Right, I might just go and do that.' So the next day he went down to the funeral and it was a church with a grave yard next to it. He didn't know anything about the person getting buried, but he was there for the service. Then when the whole crowd came out, there were people there inviting each other for New Year. But nobody came to speak to him at all.

'Ach,' he said, 'I think they're queer folk, these.' So he walked along the drive and just at the edge, near the grass, he saw this bone. He gave it a kick. 'Nobody invited me,' he said, 'and I canna invite them because I don't know them. So I'll invite you!'

So he went home. Now, Hogmanay passed. The next day was New Year and he was up early to look to the animals and take a round of the sheep. And the housekeeper was up and she looked through the window. 'Oh, there's somebody coming,' she said. 'Who would it be?'

He said, 'I don't know anybody here.'

This man came to the door. The housekeeper met him and took him in. 'Glad to see you,' she said, 'nice of you to come.' She didna know him. He was an oldish man, looked pretty old. He came in. The master of the house took out a bottle of whisky and gave him a dram and took one himself. The housekeeper was busy in the kitchen, getting the dinner ready, and for New Year's Day it would be a big dinner, there'd be plenty o' good things in it, I'm sure.

The two men were sitting at the table but there wasn't much conversation. The housekeeper set the table and took them in the dinner and she went back to the kitchen. They sat down, but just as the host was going to take something himself, it vanished. The food on the table was gone, there wasn't one crumb left, just empty plates. The host called the housekeeper and said, 'More food please, dear,' and some food came but once it went on the table, it vanished. There were only the plates left. 'My God,' he said to himself, 'I'd rather keep you for a week than a fortnight!'

Anyway, the housekeeper beckoned to the crofter to come into the kitchen. 'There's hardly any food left,' she said. 'That's the second lot I've brought out but who's taking it, where's it going? There's only left what'll make the breakfast tomorrow.'

'I tell you what,' said the crofter, 'make two oat bannocks, and cross them, make the mark of a cross on the top of them.' So she made them and put them on the table.

'Go on,' said the host, 'help yourself to those oatcakes.'

The man looked at them and said, 'No I'll not, I've had enough now.' He said, 'I can't take any more. It's getting late. I think I'll go.'

'How did you come here? I don't know anybody in this parish.'

'You invited me.'

'I invited you?' said the crofter. 'I never saw you before in my life. I'm only a week here, and I was at a funeral yesterday and I saw some of the neighbours, but I wasn't in conversation with them and I don't know anything about them. So, no, I don't know you, I don't know anybody here.'

'Ah well,' says the stranger, 'you invited me. And when you invite me, I always come.'

'I don't mind of it,' said the crofter. 'When did I invite you?'

'You were at a funeral, and you were walking out the drive to the road.'

'Yes,' said the crofter.

'And there was a bone beside the drive, and you kicked it, and you said "No-body invited me, so I'll invite you!" That was me; that was my bone that you kicked. Now I'm going off. You'll come a bit of the road with me. I spent the day wi' you, surely you can spend the night wi' me?'

'Well,' said the crofter, 'I've to be up early tomorrow, so I can't stay the night wi' you, but I'll go a bit of the road wi' you.' The crofter took his stick, and they set off together down the hill.

After a while the crofter said, 'I'll be going back now, I have to be getting back.'

'Well,' said the stranger, 'when you leave me, take care of yourself. And where are you going anyway?'

'Where am I going? I'm going back home.'

'Well, you might see where your house once was; but you've no cattle, no sheep, no housekeeper, you've nothing left.'

'But what happened?'

'There's a green knoll where your house used to be. You have been a long time wi' me.'

'What do you mean? There's only about five minutes since we left my house!'

'Oh yes, maybe five minutes to you,' he said, 'but I'm afraid there's nobody in this place now that you'll know. There's nobody that'll mind you. So, watch yourself.'

The crofter started to go back up the hill, and the stick that he had in his hand went into mist, the clothes came off him in tatters, he was blind and he was almost deaf. He fell into a ditch and then he heard a noise. 'I think I'm near a school,' he said to himself. 'That's the merriment of children I'm hearing.' And then the children came down and saw him – and they ran right back to the headmaster. He came down, and other people too, to see this queer man. So they took him up to one of the classrooms in the school and laid him down. The doctor came and two polis men came and had a look at him. 'What's wrong with him?'

'Nothing,' said the doctor, 'it's just old age. That man, I don't know how old he is.'

There was an old man, one of the oldest parishioners. They fetched him down to the school.

'Can you say anything about this man?' asked the doctor.

'Nothing,' he said, 'But I heard my grandfather saying that his father told him that on a New Year's Day night a crofter who was new to the parish left with a stranger who was very queer-looking. Where did they go that night? Nobody ever saw the crofter again. But I think this might be him returned.'

Well, the doctor went over again. He couldn't find anything wrong with the man, just that he was old, old, old. And they never found out the truth, because the man died.

And that's the story of the man who kicked the bone at Hogmanay.

9

A GUID
NEW YEAR

From the sixteenth century Yule pot-bangers, to the Pitsligo thiggers, to the Dingwall Crate's 'jazz' band, to today's city street parties: music, verse, song, dance and just plain noise have been an essential part of midwinter celebrations.

Robert Fergusson's poem *The Daft-Days* was published in 1772. In its verses Fergusson, who died in an asylum aged twenty-four, exhorts the citizens of Edinburgh to dance, drink, and be merry during the dark days of Yule, and tells fiddlers to tune up properly and play good, plain Scottish music:

> Fiddlers, your pins in temper fix,
> And roset weel your fiddle-sticks;
> But banish vile Italian tricks
>   Frae out your *quorum*,
> Nor *fortes* wi *pianos* mix –
>   Gie's *Tulloch Gorum*.

In 1879, the *Ross-shire Journal* reported:

> In Dingwall there was more than normal stir. The year was ushered in with an abundance of music, a flute band and a band with three pipers parading the streets. In the forenoon a brass band also turned out.

The *Press and Journal*, on 2 January 1901, described the intriguingly contrasting timbres that welcomed in the New Year in Burghead:

> The Parish Bell rang out merrily for a few minutes and the youth of the town paraded the streets with horns and whistles. A few clavies were burned.

In remote places, in the sparest of circumstances, people have assembled to put their creative mark on the turning of the year. In *The Statistical Account of Scotland* of 1793, the minister presiding over the Orkney island of North Ronaldsay reports:

> There is a large stone, about 9 or 10 feet high, and 4 broad, placed upright in a plain … The writer of this has seen 50 of the inhabitants assembled there on the first day of the year, and dancing with moon light, with no other music than their own singing.

Many families made their own Hogmanay music. Folk singer, musician and author Alison McMorland recalls her childhood in Lanarkshire in the 1940s:

> My mother played the fiddle – I remember her playing for us to dance to. And our family was very much one where singing would happen at the drop of a hat, there was no holding back about not doing a song. So everyone would do turns at New Year, with songs going around the room. My father always said that my grandparents used to sing *Huntingtower*; that was their Ne'er Day turn.

Alison worked with Willie Scott, born in the Scottish Borders in 1897, to record memories of his life as a shepherd and singer. Willie's recollections of youthful Guising at Hogmanay – or Auld Year's Nicht as he called it – were closely bound up with song:

> We were aa disguised an A sung in a Northumberland twang so's they widnae ken whae A wes; an A played the fiddle and they'd mebbe do a Hielan Scottische – or anything A'd a mind tae play, they'd dance. The sang A sung wes *Bound Tae Be A Row* – Oh, A learnt that afore A left the schuil. *Mistress Paxton's Shop* wes a great favourite o Frances, ma wife, that wes her pairty piece, that an *Bonnie Wee Trampin Lass*, on Auld Year's Nicht.

Children have their own New Year songs, as we've seen. Words like 'Rise up guid wife, and binna sweir …' echo repeatedly through the pages of this book, but there are others which are more reflective of the humour of the playground. Ewan McVicar, folk singer, songwriter, musician, author and storyteller, learned *Today is Hogmanay* – to the tune of *Courting in the Kitchen* – from his mother:

... so it is at least eighty years old. My mother learned the first two verses in the playground in Plean school, near Stirling, when she was eight years old, and I was eight when she taught it to me. My father added on the last verse, which is the chorus of a nineteenth-century pseudo-Gaelic song called *Phairson Swore a Feud*. Make the bagpipe sound of the 'ahs' by holding your nose with one hand and beating gently on your throat with the edge of the other hand.

Today is Hogmanay
Tomorrow's Hogmananny
And ah'm gaun doon the brae
Tae see my Irish grannie.

Ah'll tak her tae a ball
Ah'll tak her tae a supper
And when ah get her there
Ah'll stick her nose in the butter.

Singing ah ah ah, ah ah
Ah ah ah ah ah ah

Ah ah ah ah ah
And that's the Gaelic chorus.

Composing a new song at New Year was common in island communities with a strong song-making tradition. One well-known example, widely sung with many variant verses, was composed on New Year's Day in 1876 by Skye-born bard Mary MacPherson, as exiled Highlanders prepared to do battle with shinty sticks in the heart of Glasgow:

'S iad gillean mo rùin a thogadh mo shunnd;
'S i seo a'Bhliadhn' Ur thug sòlas dhuinn;
'S iad gillean mo rùin a thogadh mo shunnd.
The lads I love would lift my spirit,
This is the New Year that brought us joy.

A Lochaber farmer adapted this chorus when, the story goes, the *Gillean mo Rùin/The Lads I Love* of the title – his own seven sons – came home unexpectedly one New Year.

Company was not always necessary. Peter Morrison of Grimsay, North Uist, found himself alone at New Year in 1969, but lines in the *Oran Bliadhn' Uire/New Year Song* that he made that night tell how his cat and dog became merry on the drops of whisky he fed them. Then a phone call lifted his own spirits and the final verses wish long life, health and happiness to all his friends.

Nostalgia featured too. In *Ilean Bithidh Sunndach/Boys be Joyful*, Donald McColl, stalker in Acharacle, looked back fondly to the New Years of his youth in Ardnamurchan, marching from house to house to find a blazing fire and corks popping from the whisky bottles, pipes in full swing for the dance, and tables crammed with baked goods. But, in the years of scarcity after the Second World War, the bard concluded that, whether you liked it or not, *Tha a'Chollainn 'dol a bhàn*, 'Hogmanay is on the decline.'

Sheila Stewart, daughter of Alec and Belle of the renowned Perthshire Traveller family 'The Stewarts of Blair', recalls a family decision:

My mother and her two brothers, Andy and Donald, decided they should all always make a song for the New Year – but it had to be a song about the family or what the family did. And the first one she ever made up for New Year was *The Berryfields o' Blair* and it became her best known song.

Up until twelve o'clock everyone was in their own house – my mother made pots of food, the table was always set, and the very last thing before 12 o'clock struck was to clear the grate from under the fire and empty out the ashes. No-body had a drink before midnight but then the head of the house had to dish out the first drink. And then we'd be out first-footing to all the relatives round about. But you never went out the door that night without something on your head – 'you daurna meet the New Year wi' a bare heid', was what the Travellers said. My father would always get his pipes out at Hogmanay. Once, when we were staying in New Alyth, he walked all around the streets after midnight, playing his pipes. Everyone from round about joined in the procession – it was a real highlight!

Finally, to the songs that are associated most closely with the New Year; that we sing in chorus after the Bells, the cheering and the shaking of hands. Until Robert Burns' *Auld Lang Syne* – or at least its first verse and chorus – became universally accepted as 'the Hogmanay song', a great favourite, sung on New Year's Eve both live and on radio and television, and played by brass bands and on church bells, was *A Guid New Year To Ane An A'*, written by Peter Livingstone, who was born in a Dundee tenement in 1823. It's a generous song, whose chorus runs:

A guid New Year to ane an a',
And mony may you see,
An during a the years that come,
O happy may you be.

Livingstone, who died young at the age of twenty-eight, and whose works were published posthumously by his father, was a great Burns enthusiast – calling him 'the Scottish Shakespeare' – and the text of *A Guid New Year* has direct echoes of *Auld Lang Syne*. Both songs evoke an idyllic rural childhood, playing among the burns and braes. But, while Burns celebrates the pleasure of meeting an old friend over a drink, after a long separation, Livingstone is more melancholy, wondering whether:

… ilka ane
I see sae happy here,
Will meet again and happy be
Anither guid New Year?

Burns' song was first published in 1796, shortly after his death. It was, as the poet freely admitted, built around a lyric that already existed; in 1788 he wrote in a letter how it was inspired by 'an old song and tune which has often thrilled thro' my soul'. Elsewhere he claimed to have taken it down from the singing of an old man. However little or much Burns contributed to them, here are the words – spare, direct and affecting – as they appear in James Johnson's *Scots Musical Museum*, to a tune more plangent and reflective than the one generally used today, and with a note saying that 'some sing Kiss, in place of Cup':

Should auld acquaintance be forgot
And never brought to mind?
Should auld acquaintance be forgot,
And auld lang syne!

Chorus:
For auld lang syne, my jo,
　For auld lang syne,
We'll tak a cup o' kindness yet
　For auld lang syne.

And surely ye'll be your pint stowp!
　And surely I'll be mine!
And we'll tak a cup o' kindness yet,
　For auld lang syne.
　　For auld, &c.

We twa hae run about the braes,
　And pou'd the gowans fine;
But we've wander'd mony a weary fitt,
　Sin' auld lang syne.
　　For auld, &c.

We twa hae paidl'd in the burn,
　Frae morning sun till dine;
But seas between us braid hae roar'd,
　Sin' auld lang syne.
　　For auld, &c.

And there's a hand, my trusty fiere!
　And gie's a hand o' thine!
And we'll tak a right gude-willie waught,
　For auld lang syne.
　　For auld, &c.

Pausing only to reflect that a 'gude-willie waught' means something like 'a draught of good friendship', I would like to add my own favourite to the songs of the New Year. First published in 1827, James Hogg's *Goodnight and Joy*, was, like *Auld Lang Syne*, adapted from earlier texts, verses in a venerable lineage of songs of farewell:

The year is wearin' to the wane
　An' day is fading west awa',
Loud raves the torrent an' the rain,
　And dark the cloud comes down the shaw;
But let the tempest tout an' blaw

Upon his loudest winter horn,
Good night, an' joy be wi' you a',
  We'll maybe meet again the morn!

O we hae wandered far and wide
  O'er Scotia's hills, o'er firth an' fell,
An' mony a simple flower we've cull'd,
  An' trimmed them wi' the heather-bell!
We've ranged the dingle an' the dell
  The hamlet an' the baron's ha'
Now let us take a kind farewell,
  Good night, an' joy be wi' you a'!

Though I was wayward, you were kind,
  And sorrow'd when I went astray;
For O, my strains were often wild
  As winds upon a winter's day.
If e'er I led you from the way,
  Forgie your Minstrel aince for a';
A tear fa's wi' his parting lay,
  Good night, and joy be wi' you a'!

BIBLIOGRAPHY

Black, Ronald (ed.), *The Gaelic Otherworld: John Gregorson Campbell's Superstitions of the Highlands and Islands of Scotland and Witchcraft and Second Sight in the Highlands and Islands* (Edinburgh, 2005)

Black, Ronald (ed.), *To the Hebrides: Samuel Johnson's Journey to the Western Islands of Scotland and James Boswell's Journal of a Tour to the Hebrides* (Edinburgh, 2007)

Browne, John Hutton, *The Golden Days of Youth: A Fife Village in the Past* (Edinburgh, 1893)

Carmichael, Alexander, *Carmina Gadelica Vol.1* (Edinburgh and London, 1928)

Chambers, Robert (ed.), *The Book of Days* (2 volumes, London & Edinburgh, 1878)

Chambers, Robert (ed.), *Popular Rhymes of Scotland* (3rd Edition, London & Edinburgh, 1841; 3rd Edition with additions, Edinburgh, 1847)

Cowie, Robert, *Shetland: Descriptive and Historical; and Topographical Description of that County* (Aberdeen, 1879)

Cumming, C. F. Gordon, *In the Hebrides* (Edinburgh, 1883)

Cunningham, Allan, *The Works of Robert Burns with His Life Vol.V* (London, 1834)

Daiches, David (ed.), *A Companion to Scottish Culture* (London, 1981)

Douglas, Hugh, *The Hogmanay Companion* (Glasgow, 1999)

Edmonston, Thomas, 'Notes' in *Proceedings of the Society of Antiquaries of Scotland* (June 1870)

Fergusson, R. Menzies, *Rambles in the Far North* (1884)

Gilchrist, Anne G., 'Sacred Parodies of Secular Folk Songs: a Study of the Gude and Godlie Ballates of the Wedderburn Brothers' in the *Journal of the English Folk Dance and Song Society*, Vol.3, No.3, Dec.1938

Gorrie, Daniel, *Summers and Winters in the Orkneys* (London, 1869)

Gregor, Walter, *Notes on the Folk-Lore of the North-East of Scotland* (1881)

Hayward, Brian, *Galoshins: The Scottish Folk Play* (Edinburgh, 1992)

Jacob, Violet, *Songs of Angus* (London, 1915)

Jamieson, John (ed.), *Etymological Dictionary of the Scottish Language* (2 Volumes), (Edinburgh, 1808 & 1809)

Keay, John & Julia (eds), *Collins Encyclopaedia of Scotland* (1994)

Laing, Alexander, *Lindores Abbey and its Borough of Newburgh: their history and annals* (Edinburgh, 1876)

Lyle, Emily (ed.), *Galoshins Remembered* (Edinburgh, 2011)

McCarthy, Angela, *Scottishness and Irishness in New Zealand since 1840* (Manchester, 2011)

Maclagan, Robert Craig, *The Games and Diversions of Argyleshire* (London, 1901)

MacLennan, Hugh Dan, 'Shinty: Some Facts and Fiction in the Nineteenth Century' in *Transactions of the Gaelic Society of Inverness* Volume LIX (Inverness, 1997)

MacLeod, Norman, *Morvern: A Highland Parish* (Edinburgh, 2002)

McMorland, Alison (ed.), *Herd Laddie o' the Glen: Songs of a Border Shepherd* (2006)

McNeill, F. Marian, *The Silver Bough Vol.3: A Calendar of Scottish National Festivals, Hallowe-en to Yule* (Glasgow, 1961)

McNeill, F. Marian, *The Silver Bough Vol.4: The Local Festivals of Scotland* (Glasgow, 1968)

McPherson, J. M., *Primitive Beliefs in the Northeast of Scotland* (Aberdeen, 1929)

MacTaggart, John, *The Scottish Gallovidian Encyclopaedia* (1824)

Martin, Martin, *A Description of the Western Islands of Scotland circa 1695* (new edition, 1934)

Opie, Iona & Peter, *The Lore and Language of Schoolchildren* (London, 1977)

The Hudson's Bay Record Society, *Rae's Arctic Correspondence 1844-55* (London, 1953)

Saxby, Jessie M. E. *Shetland Traditional Lore* (Edinburgh, 1932)

Simpkins, John Ewart, *County Folk-lore, Volume VII, concerning Fife With Some Notes On Clackmannan and Ross-shire* (1914)

Smith, Donald, *Storytelling Scotland* (Edinburgh, 2001)

Stewart, W. Grant, *The Popular Superstitions and Festive Amusements of the Highlanders of Scotland* (Edinburgh, 1823; reprinted London, 1970)

The New Statistical Account of Scotland, Ministers of respective parishes (1834-1845)

The Statistical Account of Scotland, Ministers of respective parishes (1791-1792)

Tocher Journal of the Department of Celtic and Scottish Studies, University of Edinburgh (see Acknowledgements for reference details)

The internet is a splendid resource for information about Hogmanay customs. Many of the books cited above – fairly obscure publications from the nineteenth and early twentieth centuries – are available in facsimile online, and there are dozens of videos of events like the Burghead Clavie, the Biggar Bonfire, the Stonehaven Fireballs and the Comrie Flambeaux.

Enterprising readers might like to consider reviving some of the more sociable Hogmanay customs, perhaps even mounting their own production of the Galoshins play.

If you enjoyed this book, you may also be interested in…

Highland Folk Tales

BOB PEGG

The Highlands of Scotland are teeming with ancient tales that are still told today. They range from the human – great and gory battles and encounters with the last wolves in Britain – to the supernatural. Waterhorses stalk the landscape, while the sidl – the fairy people – make their homes in the green hills. In this vivid journey through the Highlands, the author leads you through the rich landscape, encountering ghosts, mermaids, an the Fuath – Scotland's very own Bigfoot.

978 0 7524 6090 1

The Little Book of Edinburgh

GEOFF HOLDER

A funny compendium packed full of frivolous, fantastic and frankly bizarre information, *The Little Book of Edinburgh* is a unique guide to the city that no one will want to be without. Unusual punishments, eccentric inhabitants, famous sons and daughters along with hundreds of startling facts An engaging mix of historical and contemporary factoids, Geoff Holder's handy little guide will ensure that you will never see Edinburgh in the same way again!

978 0 7524 8630 7

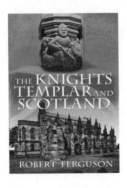

The Knights Templar and Scotland

ROBERT FERGUSON

Scotland's Knights Templar - who they were and what they has been touched upon, but never properly explored until n In *The Knights Templar and Scotland* Robert Ferguson intervi Templar and Scottish history, from the foundation of the ore in the early twelfth century right up to the present day. This essential book for anyone with an interest in the history of Knights Templar.

978 0 7524 9338 1

Visit our website and discover thousands of
other History Press books.

www.thehistorypress.co.uk

The
History
Press